I Hear You

D0376321

I Hear You

A Listening Skills Handbook
Revised Edition

Eastwood Atwater

Walker and Company
New York

First published in the United States of America in 1992
by Walker Publishing Company, Inc.

Published simultaneously in Canada by Thomas Allen & Son
Canada, Limited, Markham, Ontario

Library of Congress Cataloging-in-Publication Data
Atwater, Eastwood.
I hear you : a listening skills handbook / Eastwood Atwater.—
Rev. ed.
p.   cm.
Includes bibliographical references and index.
ISBN 0-8027-7362-1
1. Communication in management.
2. Communication in industrial
relations.   I. Title
HD30.3.A9   1992
658.4′52—dc20   91-22429
CIP

Printed in the United States of America

1   2   3   4   5   6   7   8   9   10

Chart on p. 20 reproduced by permission of McGraw-Hill, Inc.

Material presented on pp. 46, 49, 51, and 59 adapted by
permission of Brooks/Cole Publishing Company,
Pacific Grove, Calif. 93950. All rights reserved.

Contents

Foreword

Shortly after midnight one cold North Atlantic spring, the third officer on a small passenger liner dropped by the wireless office to see what messages might be going out from other ships, including a big liner stopped about ten miles away. The regular wireless operator had gone off duty, so the officer put on the headphones and listened. He had become rather good at deciphering the dots and dashes, but tonight he heard nothing. He didn't know that the primitive clockwork mechanism running the wireless had to be wound by hand. If he had done that, he could have heard the distress calls of the *Titanic* in time to save fifteen hundred lives. It was an extreme example of what can befall us when we don't know how to listen.

Listening failures are many and, for better or for worse, we can seldom blame them on technology. As Dr. Eastwood Atwater points out in this valuable work, it generally comes down to simple inability or unwillingness to collect, decipher, and retain the spoken words being offered to us. In American business today we are reaping the results of too many past failures to listen as well as we might have to our customers at home and around the globe. Few of us now, in these complex and challenging times, need further convincing of the urgent need to listen. Dr. Atwater's particular gift to our future is to tell us in sprightly and understandable terms how to go about it.

When the company for which I work began a training program called "Listening Naively," *I Hear You* was the prime item of recommended reading. To our dismay, we found that all of the available copies had been sold and the book had gone out of print. Dr. Atwater graciously allowed us to make photocopies enough to continue our training program, but that was not the end of the story.

"Out of print" is usually the epitaph for a book, and as supervisor of acquisitions for a major corporate library I see them come and go with dizzying regularity. For most out-of-print books, it really is "The End," but a few of the best ones come back. These are the ones whose message stands the test of time. Happily, this has been the fate of *I Hear You*, and it is back among us in a revised and expanded edition, ready for heavy and serious use.

In ordering the book for our company, our concern was primarily with listening as a vital business tool, but the applications go beyond the office into relationships of every sort. It is time for all of us to wind the clockwork of our own mental wireless and listen actively to what Dr. Atwater has to say. We will all benefit and so will our coworkers, customers, friends, and family. We never know, for that matter, when there might be another *Titanic* just over the horizon.

—Jerry Eckrom
Weyerhaeuser Company
Tacoma, Washington

Preface

Of all the communication skills, listening is the earliest learned and the most frequently used. Yet it is the least taught and the least mastered. Although we spend more than one-half of our communication time listening, much of it is wasted because we listen so poorly.

In the workplace, individuals are promoted to management positions on the basis of their specialized skills and performance. It is assumed they will learn human relations skills on the job, but many of them don't. As a result, one of the most common criticisms of workers and managers alike is, "My boss doesn't listen to me."

Much that is written on the subject simply stresses the importance of listening. This book is unique in that it focuses on *how* to listen. Throughout the following pages we will explain the attitudes and techniques for effective listening, together with suggestions for improving your listening habits. The dos and don'ts of listening are summarized in the final chapter as a handy guide for your future reference.

I'm indebted to Carl Rogers, the founder of person-centered psychology, for my interest in listening. Rogers led the year-long practicum in person-centered counseling that was part of my doctoral program at the University of Chicago. In turn, I want to thank the many students and clients who have furthered and enriched my development in this area. I also greatly appreciate the generous and thoughtful help of my wife, Kay, throughout the writing of this book.

Whatever Happened to Listening?

How much of our waking day is spent in listening? We're awakened by the alarm clock, hear the weather report on the radio or television, speak and listen to other family members at breakfast, say hello to neighbors on the way to work, hum along with a song on a Walkman or the car radio, and engage in conversation with our colleagues at the office. If you kept a record, you would probably discover that you send and receive hundreds of spoken or other aural messages during the course of a day.

An ancient sage once said, "We have been given two ears and but a single mouth, in order that we may listen more and talk less." In practice, however, only about half of our communication time is spent in listening. Of course, this depends on one's work and family roles and interactions. Traditional teachers spend a large portion of their time speaking, while students usually do most of the listening. Parents of small children and daycare-center workers spend an even greater part of their communication time listening. In business, success at all levels may well depend on how well you listen to detailed instructions or to feedback from your staff. Yet the most common criticism of managers is that they don't listen.[1]

Despite the amount of time spent in listening, the average person does not listen very well. Immediately after hearing someone talk, we generally understand and remember only about half of what was said. Within the next forty-eight hours we forget half of that again, so that we retain only 25 percent of what we originally heard. Failure to listen is reflected in off-the-cuff remarks such as "I just told you. Weren't you listening?" Or "Maybe you missed what I said last week. Here it is again."

How Well Do You Listen?

Do you ever just pretend to be listening and then have to ask people to repeat what they have said? Do you frequently misunderstand what you have heard?

To find out how well or poorly you listen, you might try this: The next time someone initiates a conversation with you, ask yourself, "Am I really listening or am I thinking of what I want to say next?" With a corner of your awareness take stock of your own mental processes. Are you:

- ☐ faking attention, or acting polite?
- ☐ straying from the speaker's message?
- ☐ reacting to emotional words?
- ☐ interrupting frequently?
- ☐ tuning out uninteresting topics?
- ☐ daydreaming, if the speaker is slow?
- ☐ jumping to conclusions?
- ☐ finding fault with the message?
- ☐ thinking of what you want to say?

The more of these you find yourself doing while someone is talking to you, the less you are listening. Try this several times and see how you do. You may surprise yourself.

If you have difficulty doing this while someone is talking to you, try doing it just after the conversation, while it is still fresh in your mind. Or try doing it on the telephone, when you won't be distracted by facial expressions, eye contact, or body language. Do you take notes when you are on the phone?

Use this simple exercise to become more aware of your listening habits, especially the difficulty of listening well.

Among people who have been asked to rate themselves as listeners, more than 85 percent rate themselves as *average or worse*. Fewer than 5 percent rate themselves as "superior" or "excellent."[2] How would you rate yourself as a listener? How do you think others would rate you? Ask a friend, someone at work, or your spouse or child for their opinions.

Faulty Listening Habits

Often we fail to listen well for some rather obvious reasons. Many times we are too busy talking to listen, or we may be preoccupied or distracted. Sometimes we are simply too tired or too lazy to listen. After all, listening is hard work because it requires concentration. But most often it's because of our faulty listening habits.

Think of the worst listeners you know and describe their listening habits. Robert L. Montgomery found that the poor listener:

- □ always interrupts
- □ jumps to conclusions
- □ finishes the speaker's sentences
- □ is inattentive
- □ changes the subject
- □ writes everything down
- □ doesn't give any responses
- □ is impatient
- □ loses his or her temper
- □ fidgets nervously[3]

Sound familiar? Probably so, because each of us has engaged in some of these practices at one time or another. However, when we exhibit any of these at least 40 percent of the time, others tend to see them as habitual or characteristic of us. Let's look more closely at some of these habits.

1. Interrupting. It's no surprise that this one tops the list because it's usually very rude to interrupt. A possible exception would be when you're conversing with a compulsive talker who won't let you "get a word in edgewise." Then too, people characterized as having a high involvement style of communication not only interrupt more, but don't mind being interrupted. But most people don't like to be interrupted. Doing so habitually is a way of saying, "You're not important. Listen to *me*." But who wants to be treated that way?

In an animated exchange, listeners frequently interject a brief comment and then make a retrieval response that reestablishes the speaker's prior subject, without interrupting the flow of conversation. However, less considerate listeners often interrupt to change the subject, which does disrupt the flow of conversation. Changing the subject without mutual consent is a way of controlling or dominating the conversation. When two or more individuals keep switching from one subject to another, the conversation resembles a tug of war. The content of the conversation becomes disjointed, and each participant goes away feeling frustrated and wondering what has happened, apart from the fact of their meeting.

Another reason for interrupting people is the widespread preference for talking over listening. Too often listening is mistakenly seen as submissiveness or a surrender of control in a conversation. Interrupting, or the attempt to gain the talking role, becomes a sign of dominance. For instance, when individuals of different social statuses are conversing, such as a boss and a worker, the higher status person is not only more likely to initiate communication but also to interrupt the other person.

2. Jumping to conclusions. When six-year-old David asked his mother, "Where did I come from?" she winced, sighed, and proceeded to tell him the facts of life—how babies are conceived and born. But when she had finished, her son said, "Well, John told me he and his family came from Chicago, and I wanted to know where we came from." Having jumped to a conclusion about the meaning of his question, the mother unnecessarily put herself into a difficult situation and answered a completely different question.

Jumping to conclusions may arise from the gap in the rates of speed for thought and speech. Ordinarily, people speak at about 120 to 180 words per minute, though we can listen at about three to four times that rate, up to 800 words a minute.[4] Although this speech-thought gap provides the conscientious listener with a time advantage for listening, it tends to work against those who are less attentive to the speaker's words. It allows the listener's mind to run ahead of the speaker's words and indulge in all kinds of mental trips. Also, it may prompt poor listeners to anticipate what the speaker is *going* to say and begin formulating an answer, while missing what is *being* said.

We also jump to conclusions because of our habit of judging too quickly. It seems that we have a natural tendency to judge, evaluate, and approve or disapprove the statements of other people. For instance, if a friend begins telling us about a movie she's recently seen, our initial response is likely to be, "Did you like it?" "Was it any good?" Such judgmental questions interfere with good listening. Evaluation has an important place in listening, but later in the process. *First*, we listen to understand. *Only then* may we evaluate what we hear. Whenever we jump to conclusions we miss valuable information and end up misunderstanding what we hear.

3. Hurrying the speaker. Probably the most obvious listening fault is finishing the speaker's sentences. For instance, someone says, "I've reconsidered the matter, and I've decided to . . ." at which point the listener interrupts to say ". . . Quit, right?" "No," replies the speaker, somewhat annoyed. "What I was going to say is that I've decided to stay." When this happens we usually feel foolish, don't we? Compulsive talkers, in particular, are likely to finish the speaker's sentences, or those who are familiar with the speaker's attitudes, habits, and often-told stories. This is especially likely to occur between old friends, co-workers, and spouses, though it's rarely appreciated.

And then there's the "hurry sickness." We live at a very fast pace today and many of us are overextended. In our attempts to get more out of our lives we try to crowd more things into less time, so we're often in a hurry. As a result, we become impatient very easily and are especially apt to rush someone who speaks slowly, is inarticulate, or gets bogged down in irrelevant details.

4. Listening passively. Observe two people engaged in animated conversation and you'll probably notice that both of them continue to be active when they assume the listening role. Good listeners spontaneously tend to make various minimal responses, such as "oh," "yeah," and "really?" which generally enhance the flow of conversation. Good listeners also give feedback to let the speaker know they understand what is being said. But people who listen passively don't give any responses, even minimal ones that encourage the speaker to continue. Nor do they furnish any feedback to let the speaker know they've heard them. Speakers soon lose interest in communicating to a passive listener, and passive listeners themselves risk becoming inattentive.

5. Being inattentive. Who isn't guilty of this *at least* once a day? Listening requires active concentration, which is not easy. Our thoughts may be miles away from what is being said. For example, when college students in a psychology course were asked to record their momentary thought at various times throughout the course, the results were as follows:

- ☐ 20 percent were paying attention, though only 12 percent were actively listening.
- ☐ 20 percent were pursuing erotic fantasies.
- ☐ 20 percent were reminiscing. The remaining 40 percent were daydreaming, worrying, pondering religious thoughts, or thinking about lunch.[5]

During listening, our attention ordinarily keeps "going away" and "coming back" to the speaker's message. When we're interested in what is being said we tend to stay with the speaker, but when we're uninterested or listening half-heartedly, our thoughts stray. We tend to listen passively and are easily distracted. Our eyes begin to wander, we fidget or gesture with our hands—all of which are evident to the speaker.

FAULTY LISTENING HABITS
- ☐ Inattention to the speaker
- ☐ Listening passively
- ☐ Judging the speaker prematurely
- ☐ Rushing the speaker
- ☐ Interrupting the speaker
- ☐ Changing the subject
- ☐ Becoming emotionally aroused

Which of these faulty listening habits is most characteristic of you? Do you tend to interrupt or hurry the speaker? Or are you more apt to listen passively or become inattentive? Learning to identify your own particular faults in listening is indispensable for learning to listen more effectively. Think about it!

The Hazards of Not Listening

So often it is said of someone who gets into trouble, "He simply wouldn't listen." The rebellious teenager may come to mind, or a headstrong youth who gets involved with "bad company." But many adults are equally at fault. Alice, a troubled teenager who eventually died of an overdose of drugs, had written about her parents in her diary: "They talk, and they talk and they talk and talk, but never once did they even hear one thing I was trying to say."[6] Both parents had tried to help their daughter, but, at least from Alice's point of view, they couldn't help because they didn't listen to her.

That not listening may be dangerous is dramatically illus-
trated in fatal accidents such as the sinking of the *Titanic*. We
are told that the captain and crew of the newly christened
ship refused to listen to no less than *seven* warnings of
icebergs on that fateful night of April 12, 1912. As a result,
about 1,500 people lost their lives needlessly. They had been
led to believe the *Titanic* was "unsinkable." Even after the
ship had struck an iceberg and was slowly sinking, most of
the passengers refused to heed the captain's orders to get
into lifeboats. Comfortably housed on an upright ship with a
dark, cold sea down below, they preferred to stay on board as
long as possible. When the ship finally began listing steeply
just before sinking, it was too late. The only survivors were
the people who had listened and taken to the lifeboats.

A bank in Spokane, Washington, learned an expensive
lesson about listening to customers. John Barrier, a man in
his late fifties, was wearing his usual shabby clothes when he
drove his pickup truck into the parking lot of his bank. He
made a quick visit to his broker, cashed a check in the bank,
and then walked outside to drive away. The lot attendant told
him there was a sixty-cent parking fee but that Barrier could
take his slip inside to get it validated. No problem, Barrier
thought, because he had done business with the bank for
more than thirty years. But the teller looked at his grubby
clothes and refused to stamp the parking slip. She explained
that the bank only validated parking tickets when a customer
made a transaction, but that cashing a check wasn't considered a transaction. Barrier then asked to speak to the manager, who also refused. At that point, Barrier said, "Fine, you
don't need me, and I don't need you." Then he walked over
to a cashier and withdrew all his money—totaling over *a
million dollars*. An area manager for the bank confirmed
Barrier's story and added that the incident had prompted the
bank to review the way it did business.[7]

The overall cost of faulty listening in the workplace is
staggering. It's estimated that if each of the 100 million

workers in America makes a simple ten-dollar mistake, billions of dollars will be wasted. Just think of the letters that must be retyped, the appointments that must be rescheduled, the shipments that must be reshipped, and the customers who are lost—all because someone failed to listen. When people in large corporations fail to listen to each other, the costs are magnified. Information and ideas are distorted as they travel through the chain of command. Workers feel alienated from management, and management in turn feels more distant from executives, as well as from other workers.

How You Became the Listener You Are

If you've begun to realize that you don't listen very well, take heart. You have plenty of company, for good listeners are the exception rather than the rule. First, this is because we've learned to listen by example, and most of us have grown up in homes in which good listening was not positively modeled. Second, in the process of becoming socialized we've acquired all sorts of filters or barriers to listening, such as stereotypes about people. In addition, we often pick up new filters in our careers and work settings. Becoming aware of these influences in your life will help you to discover how you became the listener you are.

The Formative Years

Our listening attitudes and behaviors are formed very early in life. A quiet baby gets little or no attention. But when this same baby cries, in comes mommy or daddy to pick him up, change him, feed him, or offer soothing words and caresses, depending on the needs of the moment. As a result, babies soon discover that making a big noise gets more attention than just lying there and listening to others make noises.

This message is reinforced thoughout the early school years, in which students are rewarded for their ability to read, speak, or write. Seldom are they praised for their ability to listen, though this in itself is a significant factor in comprehension. In my own teaching experience, I've found that students who do poorly on tests also often fail to follow instructions in providing the requested information on their answer sheets. These students seem to have difficulty listening, including paying attention and processing information accurately. The bias against listening continues throughout the adult years, partly because of the value our society places on assertiveness and self-expression. As a result, most of us prefer to talk rather than listen. Talking is a way of exerting control and gaining status, while listening often connotes inferior status and is associated with underlings.

Our listening habits are shaped partly by the parental models we've grown up with. Children tend to do what their parents *do*, not what they say. Consequently, when children see their parents simply talking *at* each other and interrupting without really listening, they learn to do the same. It may take years to recognize how their faulty listening habits were shaped by their parents. For instance, a woman once had terrible conflicts with her mother, whom she described as an authoritarian person who constantly interrupted others and dominated the conversation. Despite her antipathy to such a poor model, this woman became a compulsive talker herself, who couldn't understand why her husband never said anything!

Children who have grown up with authoritarian parents often learn poor listening habits. Such parents tend to give orders, issue threats, and interrupt their children. Their children, in turn, tend to become passive, sullen listeners— outwardly complying with authority figures, but inwardly resistant to what is being said. They may grow up automatically "tuning out" authority figures. One young man from such a home said that his parents were always criticizing or blaming someone. As a result, he had learned to "tune out" authority figures. For years he was able to sit in class without absorbing much of anything; he barely graduated from high school. Only in therapy did he become aware of his poor listening habits and modify them.

More fortunate are children who grow up in homes in

which parents are warm and accepting, who explain family rules, and invite verbal give and take. When parents listen, children feel appreciated and worthwhile. In fact, a parent's willingness to listen is the main way of showing that he or she cares deeply about the child. This is especially so in instances of disagreement or conflict, in which it is important to hear the child out rather than interrupting. Such behavior provides a positive model of listening for the child, who is more apt to return the favor of good listening later on. What about you? Which type of parents did you have?

The Resistance to Listening

Parents and teachers may unwittingly send negative messages about listening. Whenever I ask college students to recall some of the early messages or "scripts" they received from their parents, certain comments invariably emerge. The following are typical:

- ☐ Shut up and listen.
- ☐ Don't interrupt me.
- ☐ Children should be seen and not heard.
- ☐ Be quiet.
- ☐ Can't you see I'm talking?
- ☐ I'll tell you when to speak.
- ☐ Look at me when I'm talking to you.
- ☐ Now you listen to me.

The common theme in these messages is that listening is something you *must* do; it becomes a form of compliance. Unfortunately, when it becomes a duty, listening is associated with powerless and submissive behavior. It is natural for this feeling in a child to cause a resistance to listening. *Not* listening then becomes a defensive maneuver, a way for underlings to assert their power. The resistance to listening becomes a way of preserving one's autonomy and self-respect, though ultimately this becomes self-defeating.

As adults, it helps to become aware of any resistance to listening that may linger in our makeup. In many instances, our listening habits have been influenced by particular people and circumstances now lost to awareness. Perhaps our resistance to listening was appropriate at an earlier age. But now we need to ask ourselves, "Is my reluctance to listen still appropriate?" Or, "Has my life situation changed, making it more important to listen?"

We need to realize that we have the freedom and thus the personal right to listen or not. It's our choice. In certain instances, we may *choose* not to listen, especially when dealing with opinionated, derogatory people, but it should be a conscious choice. All too often, we fail to listen by default, because we're unaware of our earlier experiences and resistance to listening. Wiser people may heed Plutarch's advice, "Learn how to listen and you will prosper even from those who talk badly."

Listening Through Emotional Filters

A major source of faulty listening is that we listen through emotional filters. These filters consist of all kinds of attitudes, beliefs, and emotional associations we've acquired in the process of growing up and becoming socialized. These become internalized in our self-concept, or the way we see ourselves, and in turn affect the way we perceive the world and process information. Consequently, we hear what we're *prepared* to hear, what we *need* to hear, or *want* to hear, rather than what is actually being said. When we have difficulty getting someone to understand us, we may say, "I'm having trouble getting through to you," implying a certain resistance due to their emotional filters. But do people sometimes say the same of you?

Some of the filters that exert the greatest impact on listening include:

☐ Attitudes   ☐ Memories
☐ Aspirations   ☐ Past experiences
☐ Assumptions   ☐ Prejudices
☐ Beliefs   ☐ Self-images
☐ Expectations   ☐ Sex roles
☐ Feelings (intense)   ☐ Unfulfilled needs
☐ Interests   ☐ Values

The particular filters each of us has acquired become such an intimate part of us that we are blind (or deaf) to them. It's easy to detect other people's blind spots, but it's usually in discussion, if not disagreement, with others that we discover our own filters or blind spots. I once became acutely aware of this when I was conducting a class session on prejudice. I explained that everyone has certain prejudices, depending largely on where and how they grew up. The most important thing is to become aware of our own particular prejudices and, short of ridding ourselves of them, to make allowances for such emotional filters in order that we may listen more objectively. During the discussion that followed, one student said, "I don't see why you're talking about prejudice with us, when it's the people *over* thirty that have all the prejudice." The class roared with laughter. When the laughter subsided, I asked, "Might that remark itself reflect a prejudice—against older people?"

The presence of emotional filters probably accounts for the wide variation in our listening ability, depending on *who* is talking and *what* is being discussed. Hence training in listening skills often entails identifying those words or topics that arouse our emotions, making it difficult for us to listen well. Individuals discover what "flash" words or attitudes most interfere with their listening. For instance, in recounting her experiences in a listening seminar, Gail Gregg discovered that she is a pretty good listener in professional situations in which she is conducting an interview or taking notes during a speech.[1] However, she also discovered that she was less effective in those situations when "emotional triggers" tripped her up. She became aware that she has difficulty listening to people whose appearance is strange, or who exhibit an abrupt or awkward manner, or use offensive phrases such as "you girls." She also came to realize that she, too, thwarts the communication process by injecting her own opinions and concerns into a conversation before hearing the other person out.

Are you aware of some of the emotional triggers that interfere with your listening? Are there certain types of people, such as authority figures, that you find it difficult to listen to? Are there topics you have trouble discussing in a calm, objective way? Awareness of the emotional filters acquired in our different environments will help us to listen more effectively.

Filters in the Workplace

Given the time we spend on our jobs, it's not surprising that we pick up certain filters in the workplace. Although individual differences in listening ability generally exceed any particular category, such as age or sex, listening habits vary to some extent by one's field of endeavor.

For instance, how well individuals prepare for job interviews varies somewhat according to their occupation. Although salespeople may be able to sell products, they often have difficulty selling themselves. This may be because they make their living talking, and they believe they can talk their way through any situation. As a result, they often fail to prepare adequately for job interviews. Apparently, some salespeople get so carried away with talking during the interview that they fail to listen to and answer questions adequately. Lawyers and advertising people have similar problems. Among those who do best in job interviews are engineers and financial planners. Engineers tend to benefit from their tendency to do advance planning, and financial planners utilize their concern for accuracy and detail to provide the specific, factual answers interviewers want.[2]

In one survey, consumers were asked to score (on a scale of one to ten with ten being the highest) a variety of health professionals on their willingness to listen. Not surprisingly, health professionals whose job includes listening to people's feelings and problems scored relatively high: psychiatrists (8.4), clinical psychologists (7.5), family practitioners (7.4), and registered nurses (7.1). Health professionals who dealt more directly with bodily concerns scored somewhat lower on their willingness to listen, with podiatrists and physical therapists scoring about 2.9.[3]

The willingness to listen, or not, can have tremendous implications on job performance. The Federal Aviation Administration (FAA) has estimated that up to eight out of ten commercial airline accidents are partially due to "human factors." A major cause is the inability to listen. Airline captains often learn to fly as military pilots, yet their military training does not prepare them to be effective managers of a crew in the cockpit of a commercial airline. For instance, in the 1982 Air Florida accident, the voice recorder revealed that the copilot had warned the captain *four* times before takeoff that something was wrong, but the captain didn't really listen. After struggling to take off with excessive ice on the wings, the plane hit the Fourteenth Street Bridge in Washington, D.C., and plunged into the Potomac River. Seventy-eight people lost their lives.[4]

To overcome such problems, many airlines are introducing Cockpit Resource Management into pilot training. The purpose is to improve communication and cooperation among flight crews. Captains of planes are regarded as managers. Since they often meet their crew for the first time only an hour before takeoff, they need to establish both their authority and their receptiveness to advice. In the past, pilots were hired for their technical skills and learned human relations skills on the job. Now this program is attempting to teach the importance of communication and cooperation as well as technical skills.[5]

A similar observation can be made among managers in other areas in the workplace. In their book *Problem Bosses*, Peter Wylie and Marcey Grothe report that the two most common faults they hear are: "My boss doesn't listen to me" and "My boss doesn't give me good feedback." Apparently, a lot of bosses are terrible listeners. They talk nonstop, interrupt others, and don't show much regard for their workers' thoughts and feelings. This is because promotions are awarded primarily on the basis of technical skill and performance. Like pilots, managers are expected to learn human relations skills on the job, but many of them don't.[6]

What about you? Are you fortunate enough to have a boss or supervisor who listens? Or is he or she a poor listener? Whether this is a problem or not, you might turn the tables and ask yourself "How well do *I* listen?" As we've seen throughout this chapter, most of us do not listen well because of the way we've learned to listen. The next several chapters focus on developing the skills for better listening. As you learn to use these skills, you might try listening to your boss first as a way of getting your boss to listen to you.

3

Learning to Listen

Are you aware that listening is the earliest communication skill acquired, the most often used, but the least mastered? Through listening, along with the other senses, infants comprehend much of what their parents are communicating to them, as early as the first few months of life. Infants become attentive listeners long before they are able to express themselves by speaking, which generally occurs in their second year of development. Yet, as we've seen, children generally acquire poor listening habits because of faulty role modeling on the part of their parents. In addition, a certain resistance to listening often develops as a result of the negative messages equating listening with passive compliance.

Unfortunately, the lack of training in listening is compounded when children begin school. Throughout the years of formal schooling, students spend 50 percent or more of their communication time in listening, followed by speaking, reading, and writing in that order. However, the amount of training time students receive in these skills occurs in just the reverse order. For instance, college students receive the most training in writing, followed by reading and speaking in that order. They receive the least training in listening.

The good news is that since listening is learned, our faulty listening habits can be retrained. Although there has been less systematic training in listening by comparison to the other communication skills, we know that listening skills can be improved. People who read books on listening, participate

Distribution of Communication Activities by Frequency of Use and Instruction

Adapted from Lyman K. Steil, Larry L. Barker, and Kittie W. Watson, *Effective Listening: Key to Your Success*. New York: Random House, 1983, p. 5.

in seminars on listening, and take courses in communication skills generally acquire greater awareness of the listening process and begin improving their listening skills. In some instances, especially in seminars and courses devoted to the subject, listening comprehension has as much as doubled in a few months.[1]

Today, virtually everyone could benefit from improved listening skills. People in the helping and service professions, such as doctors, nurses, counselors, and teachers need to listen in order to understand the people they work with. Of course, good listening habits are best begun in the home, when couples and parents practice listening and their children and adolescents grow up realizing its importance for effective communication. Nowhere is listening more critical than in the workplace, where poor communication between salespeople and their customers and management and their workers results in poor morale, low productivity, and mediocre service, as well as diminished profits.

Hearing and Listening

Perhaps a good place to begin is the distinction between hearing and listening. According to Webster's New World Dictionary, to listen is "to make a conscious effort to hear" or "to pay attention to sound." Right away, you will notice that listening involves more than hearing. Essentially, hearing pertains to the physical reception of sound; listening to the perception of *meaningful* sound. Hearing is an automatic or involuntary reaction of the senses and nervous system. In contrast, listening is a voluntary act, involving our higher mental processes as well. Listening requires concentration. You must deliberately focus your attention on the speaker and what is being said. Otherwise, you will hear only as much as you need to hear or want to hear, rather than what is actually being said, which happens all too often.

As mentioned earlier, listening is made possible because of the lag between the spoken word and the mental activity of the listener. However, the speech-hearing gap that makes listening possible in the first place can also lead us astray, so if we want to listen we must make better use of this speech-hearing gap. To genuinely listen, we must (1) pay attention to the speaker's message, (2) share responsibility for the communication, (3) use total body listening, and (4) listen appropriately, depending on the purpose of the communication and the situation at hand.

Pay Attention to the Speaker's Message

The word "pay" is most appropriate here, which implies giving something in exchange for something else. Ordinarily, we speak of paying in monetary terms, but in listening we give something even more valuable—our full attention, time, and effort—which we value even more today than in the past, when life was less hurried and complex. In return for listening we may receive accurate information, understanding, entertainment, encouragement, or comfort, and may perceive people's innermost feelings. However, to give our full attention to another person demands constant effort, which may help to explain why we do not really listen well much of the time.

Ultimately, listening is also a gift. One of the greatest gifts we can give someone is the gift of really listening to that person. Since listening requires that we give something of ourselves, it is more demanding than simply giving money, favors, or things. People who are unduly self-centered find it difficult to listen because they are so wrapped up in their own lives. Those who are more outgoing and interested in people are generally more open to others, and thus more inclined to listen.

People generally appreciate the gift of listening, though they may not always say so at the time. Those who are angry or critical invariably feel relieved once they have "gotten their feelings off their chest." After being listened to, people are generally more receptive to our suggestions and ideas. Also, they tend to form a more favorable impression of good listeners. Conversely, when people feel they have been treated unfairly and have not been heard, they are much more apt to initiate legal action. Similarly, when those who are troubled or deeply hurt feel they have not been heard, they are often willing to pay money to professional helpers in order to be heard and understood.

Share Responsibility for the Communication

Strangely enough, this statement flies in the face of a common misconception, namely that the speaker is primarily responsible for the communication. For instance, Lyman Steil and his colleagues found that over two-thirds of the adults in their listening seminars believe that the primary responsibility for communication success rests with the speaker. Barely one-quarter of them felt that such responsibility rests with the listener.[2] In contrast, Henry Thoreau once said, "It takes two to speak the truth—one to speak, and another to hear." From a somewhat different perspective, Deborah Tannen says, "Much—even most—meaning in conversation does not reside in the words spoken at all, but is filled in by the person listening."[3] Thus, each of us tends to interpret what we hear in terms of our own orientation, concerns, needs, past experience, and expectations—our emotional filters—rather than in the spirit in which the words were intended. Often we fail to exercise our responsibility as listeners because we are too tired or uninterested in what is being said, or we may have a closed mind. More often than not we are not sufficiently active in trying to understand the speaker.

For instance, one study showed a wide disparity between the physician's intended message and what patients heard. The doctor's remarks "It will only hurt a little," is taken to mean anything from a quick pinch to some discomfort. Yet over one-fifth of the patients, but only 2 percent of the doctors, said it meant a lot of pain. Furthermore, only about half the doctors and patients took the phrase "going home

from the hospital soon" to mean two to four days. Yet among
the others, three times as many patients as doctors thought it
meant "tomorrow," setting the stage for misunderstanding. A
major implication of this study is that patients should assume
more responsibility in communicating with their doctors. As
patients, we must ask questions when we do not understand
just what the doctor means.[4]

Use Total Body Listening

Whenever we're eager to hear an important announcement
or the latest gossip, we might say, "I'm all ears." This means
we intend to give the speaker our undivided attention. But
do we? To accomplish this, we must adopt a posture that
enhances listening—facing the speaker, maintaining eye contact, and paying attention. Such total body listening not only
expresses our readiness to listen, but also aids the act of
listening itself. Although we may adopt body listening unconsciously, for the most part, we can deliberately adopt these
attending skills—as they are sometimes called—to enhance
our listening behavior.

It is important to minimize the distractions that keep us
from giving the speaker our undivided attention. Trying to
listen to someone in a room where other people are conversing is very difficult. If we meet someone in a crowded place,
like an auditorium, hallway, or party, it may be wise to step
aside and seek a "quiet corner." If we are in a home, turning
off the television or stereo can greatly reduce distractions. If
we are in an office, it helps to ask someone else to answer the
telephone when it rings, or ask not to be disturbed. Nothing
is so distracting as being interrupted every few minutes by
someone's telephone or secretary. While we may be duly
impressed by how busy the other person is, we cannot help
feeling like an unwanted intruder. In such a situation, if the
speaker isn't sufficiently sensitive to these matters, the listener may ask "Is it possible to talk with you in private
without being disturbed?"

The hardest part of listening is keeping our attention focused on the speaker and what is being said. A major reason is that our attention span is short—fifteen or twenty seconds or so. This is why the images in television commercials are constantly shifting—to keep our attention. And mind you, this is true for our *visual* attention, which is our primary mode of learning. Attending to a *verbal* message is even more demanding. Much of the reason has do with the gap between the rate of speaking and rate of hearing, mentioned earlier. As a result, during listening we generally find our awareness alternately "going away" and "coming back" to the speaker's words. When we're genuinely interested in what is being said, we're more apt to stay with the speaker, but when we're tired or bored, we begin to listen half-heartedly. Our thoughts easily stray and our eyes begin to wander, all of which becomes evident to the speaker. In order to listen well, we must make a constant effort to attend to the speaker and keep "coming back" to what is being said.

Maintaining eye contact with the speaker not only shows we're interested, but also encourages the speaker to continue and, in turn, helps us to pay attention. The next time someone initiates a conversation with you, notice what both of you do with your eyes. How much does the speaker look at you? How much are you gazing back in turn? Generally, the listener looks at the speaker more than vice versa. Also, the natural, spontaneous pattern in most conversations is for each person to establish eye contact briefly, then momentarily glance aside, then reestablish eye contact, repeating this pattern throughout the conversation.

Occasionally, people read a book on body language or person perception and discover that others form a more favorable impression of us when we look them in the eye, which is generally true. But then they proceed to overdo a good thing, making the speaker (or the listener, as the case may be) feel uncomfortable. This is because constant eye contact tends to be perceived as staring, which in turn signals intrusion and hostility, especially in competitive situations. In contrast, it is better to strive for optimum rather than maximum eye contact, that which feels natural and comfortable to both parties, and is appropriate to the situation.

Since much of our communication is nonverbal, positive body language expresses our desire to listen. Sitting toward the front of your chair and leaning forward with an animated expression is a way of saying, "I'm all ears." On the other hand, slouching down in your chair expresses a casual, disinterested attitude. Standing with folded arms shows a defensive attitude, while putting hands on your hips exhibits a defiant stance. When listeners show little or no body movement, especially without eye contact, a speaker may wonder if the listener is "still there." Speakers usually prefer listeners with responsive body language, though an overly fidgety listener is generally distracting. There is also a tendency for attentive listeners to unconsciously mimic the speaker's posture and gestures, as if to say "I'm with you." Other matters, like sitting or standing too close or too far away, may also enhance or interfere with communication, and will be explored in greater detail in chapter 7, "Nonverbal Communication."

BASIC ATTENDING SKILLS
- ✔ Minimize distractions
- ✔ Pay attention to the speaker's message
- ✔ Share responsibility for the communication
- ✔ Face the speaker
- ✔ Maintain eye contact
- ✔ Use responsive body language
- ✔ Listen appropriately

Listen Appropriately

Essentially, this means taking into account the purpose of communication. People communicate for all sorts of reasons, some of which are not always clear to themselves, much less to others. Sometimes they are simply being sociable such that the effort to greet us or make small talk, or not, means more than the words themselves. So it's best not to take people's verbal messages too literally. At other times, people are primarily communicating information, which means we have to listen more carefully to their words. Then, again, people often use words to express their feelings and attitudes, which demands empathic listening skills. In still other instances, they are mostly intent on persuading us to do something. In each case, it is important that we gear our listening to the purpose of the speaker's communication. Otherwise, we're apt to misunderstand what the speaker is expressing.

We'll describe four basic purposes of communication: social, informational, expressive, and persuasive.[5] As you read, keep in mind that speakers often shift from one purpose to another without warning, or may be communicating for more than one purpose.

1. Social communication. Here, people speak primarily to acknowledge each other's presence and to maintain their relationships with each other. This usually involves a certain amount of ritual communciation, such as saying the "expected" things, engaging in "small talk," and exchanging the courtesies of everyday life. People tend to present themselves in a favorable light and avoid revealing things they do not want others to know about them. They also take it for granted that others will do the same. Thus, much of our social communication consists of the management of surface impressions, often at the cost of honest self-disclosure and satisfying communication.

Listening appropriately at this level begins with our willingness to take part in the rituals of everyday communication. The failure to do so may jeopardize our relationships with others. Sometimes all that is needed is a nonverbal response, such as a smile or a raised hand. At other times, we may be expected to speak. Social communication involves taking turns talking and listening, or at least not interrupting. It also means not taking everything we hear at face value. When someone asks, "Hi, how are you?" we're not expected to give a literal, detailed account of our moods, much less our problems. It's usually more appropriate to indicate our momentary feelings and/or current activities as succinctly and honestly as possible in a friendly manner, such as "Okay, how about you?"

2. *Informational communication.* When people shift from social to informational communication, the content of the conversation takes on increased importance. Here, the primary purpose is to convey information, meanings, or understanding. Examples would be a professor lecturing to students, a television newscaster giving the news, and a salesperson explaining a product or service.

Appropriate listening here requires an accurate reception of the content of the message. One begins by paying close attention to what the speaker is saying, but we must also process the information for meaning and retention. If you're listening to brief bits of information, such as an appointment date or street address, mental rehearsal may be sufficient, though a written note is preferable to insure accurate retention. When it comes to more complicated information and knowledge, accurate listening requires taking more organized notes. Active listening skills are often useful for sound understanding. That is, clarifying and summarizing the speaker's message may serve to further check on its accuracy and meaning, as we'll describe in the chapter on "active" listening skills.

3. *Expressive communication.* At this level of communication, people use words mostly to express their attitudes and feelings as when two individuals are sharing a happy experience or disappointment. Here, one must listen to the tone of voice, the rate of speech, the bodily posture and gestures, as well as the words themselves. This is especially the case whenever we're dealing with problematic situations, such as disputes at work or family conflicts.

As long as the speaker is expressing strong feelings of anger and hurt, it is usually wise to rely on minimal responses that will facilitate the ventilation of strong emotions. Emotionally aroused speakers are in no mood to listen. But gradually, as the intensity of feelings subsides, active listening skills are more in order to better understand the speaker's position and message. This is especially the case when someone seeks you out as a "sounding board" for understanding or making a decision. Generally though, empathic listening is the most appropriate type of listening for expressive communication; it is indispensable when you're trying to put yourself in the other person's shoes and understand what he or she is experiencing at the moment. Instead of succumbing to the temptation to say "I understand how you feel"—a well-intended but superficial response that usually evokes disagreement—it is better to *demonstrate* such understanding by reflecting the specific feelings being expressed, as explained in the chapter on empathic listening.

4. Persuasive communication. Here the speaker is attempting to persuade the listener to do something, e.g., to make a charitable donation, to serve on a committee, to purchase a product or service, or to vote for someone running for office.

In each instance, it is important to get an accurate understanding of what is being offered or asked of you. Accordingly, active listening skills are needed to clarify and confirm the message. The more complicated the request or issue at hand, the more important active listening skills become. At the same time, evaluation now plays an important role in weighing the evidence and reaching a wise decision. Also, once you make a decision one way or the other, it is important to "close the loop" of listening by appropriate action. This is especially true in the area of sales, marketing, and service, where the speakers are clients or customers with specific expectations. When a salesperson or manager says "I'll get back to you on this," and nothing happens for weeks, the customer wonders if that person really heard the request or simply forgot it. Closing the loop of listening doesn't necessarily mean you agree with the speaker or must do what is requested—it does mean acknowledging that you understand the request and will respond to it.

Since communication takes energy and effort, people usually speak for a purpose. The better you and I can discern someone's primary purpose in communicating to us, the more appropriately we can listen to that person. Even though we do not consciously pay much attention to the purpose of communication, we take our cues from a number of things. A person's role and relationship to us often determines his or her purpose in communication. In many instances, the setting or circumstances play a major role in communication. In other instances, factors such as personalities, specific occasions, or common problems provide the clues to what a speaker intends to communicate. One caution: We become so accustomed to communicating with the same individuals in familiar situations such that a shift in the type of communication or an atypical message often goes unheeded or misunderstood. Consequently, listening well to our colleagues, close friends, and loved ones is the acid test of listening.

4

Conversational Listening

Casual conversation is probably the most familiar form of communication, though not necessarily the most skilled. Ordinarily, when conversing it's desirable for each person to speak and to listen alternately, so that they may achieve mutually satisfying communication. Yet this is not always the case. All too often, a conversation turns into a contest of who gets to speak first, or the most. Typically this results in superficial understanding as well as frustration on both sides. You might take a moment to recall some of your own recent conversations. Did you have a chance to express what you wanted to say? Did you feel you were heard? Conversely, did you really listen? Did you understand what the other person was trying to say?

Conversation is more demanding than popularly thought, partly because it frequently involves more than one purpose. At the surface, conversation often serves a social purpose, as mentioned earlier. In fact, the older, root meaning of conversation is "social intercourse"—having to do with the maintenance of social relationships. Here, the *act* of speaking serves to acknowledge the presence of others, and often takes precedence over the content involved. Even when we communicate at other levels we should not forget that the *way* we speak *and* listen to each other continues to affect our relationship—an important factor in all communication. At one time or another, however, we may engage in conversation for other purposes, with informational, expressive, or persuasive communication. Thus conversation also serves as a "verbal exchange," in which a great deal of information and understanding may be shared, as in the more substantive exchanges at school or work.

In this and the next three chapters, I will describe some basic skills for improving your listening ability. These are identified and described in separate chapters for instructional purposes. In practice, however, these skills are often used together in varying combinations, depending on the people involved and the situations. For example, even though we rely on conversational listening skills for informal, social communication in which valued relationships are central, these skills are also useful in more substantive discussions, when the content of communication is more important. Similarly, while the "active" listening skills described in the next chapter are especially appropriate in ensuring accurate transmission and understanding of the content of communication, they may be equally valuable in clarifying what is expected of us in persuasive communication. Again, even though empathic listening is especially suitable for expressive communication, this too may become appropriate during persuasive communication, in negotiations and conflict management.

We'll begin by distinguishing between private and public communication and some implications of this for conversational listening, in which it is natural to listen in an active, cooperative way that creates rapport with the speaker. Ordinarily, this involves the use of minimal verbal responses and open-ended questions that enhance the flow of conversation. Two people speaking at once from time to time need not turn the conversation into a contest, though there is always the danger of this occuring when the listener's response is disruptive or switches the subject, as we shall see.

Private Versus Public Listening
In public speaking, such as the lecture, sales report, or courtroom presentation, one person speaks at a time, with

the speaker clearly controlling the verbal activity. Interested listeners are attentive, mentally processing the message, taking notes, and possibly asking questions. By contrast, in private speaking, such as a conversation between two or more friends, the verbal activity tends to be reciprocal. Each person is expected to talk and listen alternately. Ideally, all participants should feel equally free to speak or listen. Examples of private speaking would be personal conversation, small group discussion, and intimate conversations among close friends, lovers, or family members.

People may feel more comfortable in one sphere than in another. For instance, some individuals will feel more at ease in public communication and may enjoy giving speeches and speaking up at group meetings. Others may prefer informal conversations in which there is more mutual speaking and listening among two or more individuals. Sometimes these two types of communication may even be combined. For instance, a lecturer who speaks informally and invites questions and discussion encourages more mutual dialogue than in a typical formal lecture. Or one person may do all the talking in an informal conversation, making it more of a monologue than a dialogue.

What happens when two individuals begin talking at once? This is fairly common in everyday conversation and isn't necessarily bad, as we'll see later in this chapter. Much depends on *how well* the participants communicate with each other. What often happens is that people unconsciously assume the public mode of communication, unwittingly competing for the speaking role, rather than alternating the speaking and listening roles, which is more appropriate for informal, private communication. More than one authority has observed that Americans lack the ability to converse in a balanced give-and-take conversation. For instance, when two friends meet on the street, what typically happens is that each is so eager to share his or her experiences that both may begin talking at the same time. As a result, they talk *at* each other or *past* each other, rather than listening and responding to what the other has said. So the conversation becomes a competitive exercise or contest to see who gets to speak first or assume the speaker role; it's as if the act of giving information confers status on the speaker and the first person to draw a breath is declared the listener[1]—a reluctant, frustrated listener, who doesn't listen as much as await his or her turn to speak. It's as if this second person has been consigned to the more inferior role of listener, a mere underling who receives information.

The preference for the speaking role and the reluctance to share it probably reflect a variety of factors, such as differences in temperament, status, and expressiveness as well as ethnic, socioeconomic, and cultural differences. For example, individuals of high status tend to initiate conversations and do more talking than those of lower status. Also, individuals with a high-involvement communication style prefer animated communication with overlapping expressions among the participants.

Also, as Deborah Tannen has observed, there are important gender differences in respect to conversational styles, though we need to be careful not to generalize about these.[2] For instance, many men feel more comfortable in *report*-type or public communication while many women feel more comfortable in *rapport*-type or private communication. Much of this reflects the way men and women have been socialized in our country. Because of traditional sex-roles, men have tended to identify with the problem-solver role, preferring to convey information. Also, the speaker role may satisfy a man's need for dominance, control, and status associated with the traditional male role. In contrast, women traditionally have been reared as nurturers and are generally more oriented toward establishing and negotiating relationships. As such, they have tended to seek understanding rather than dominance and are more likely to be attentive listeners. As a result, women tend to listen in a more animated and cooperative way than men.

They use more enhancing responses, such as "mm-hm" and "yeah" as well as more agreeing and laughing responses, all of which tend to create rapport with the speaker. Women also ask more questions and give more feedback. In contrast, men give fewer listener responses but make more challenging responses, which tend to break the flow of conversation.

Lacking clear awareness of these matters, individuals of both sexes are prone to blame communication problems on each other, instead of on the clash of communication styles. Men tend to misconstrue women's attentiveness, on the one hand, as submissiveness, and their animated responses, on the other hand, as competitiveness. In turn, women tend to misconstrue men's preference for the speaking role as domineering and their paucity of animated listening responses as a lack of interest. However, at a time when gender roles are changing dramatically, it is well to realize that communication styles are changing too, and are always more complex than any one such factor as gender roles.

Listening to Create Rapport

Such differences in conversational styles do suggest that each of us is more apt to create rapport and mutual understanding when we converse in a more balanced give-and-take manner. This involves alternately speaking and listening by each participant, with a more animated, cooperative style of listening. Often the sharing of speaking and listening roles occurs spontaneously, with little forethought, as when two or more partners are interested in each other and in the conversation itself. We cannot, however, always assume this will occur, so it may help to be aware of what makes for mutually satisfying communication. As speakers, we can encourage reciprocal sharing by not doing all the talking and by inviting our partner's comments. As listeners, we may enhance the flow of communication by listening in a more animated, cooperative way.

The simplest way to encourage speakers is through the use

of familiar responses such as "mm-hm." Such a simple, non-obtrusive sound communicates "I'm interested." Saying "mm-hm" or simply nodding one's head generally has the effect of encouraging the speaker to continue talking. Of course, there are many other responses that can serve the same purpose. Whenever possible, use those that come to you naturally, as long as they are truly "neutral" or nonjudgmental. Some commonly used minimal responses are:

- ☐ Yeah.
- ☐ Go on.
- ☐ I see.
- ☐ Oh?
- ☐ Tell me more.
- ☐ I'd like to hear . . .
- ☐ You don't say!
- ☐ No kidding.
- ☐ Really?

Such responses help to facilitate conversation, especially in the beginning, and also provide encouragement to the speaker in a way that mere silence would not. Although silence may be very meaningful among close friends, it is often misconstrued as a sign of disinterest or rejection among people who do not know each other well. Hence the value of the *minimal* response, just enough to enhance the flow of conversation.

Sometimes, however, people may unwittingly use short responses that reflect a judgmental attitude. Examples of these are:

- ☐ Just give me three reasons.
- ☐ Aw, come on.
- ☐ Cheer up!
- ☐ Oh, it can't be that bad.

- ☐ That's not so.
- ☐ Look at it this way: . . .
- ☐ I told you that would happen.
- ☐ Why don't you forget it?

These remarks are likely to have the effect of either shutting off the flow of conversation or, in effect, putting the speaker on the defensive. Consequently, such listener responses become "roadblocks" to communication.

We should also realize that minimal responses may be more helpful in enhancing the flow of conversation in some situations than in others. Such responses may be especially useful when speakers are eager to share something with us, such as their ideas, opinions, and attitudes, and more especially to ventilate intense feelings. It is also valuable when speakers have difficulty expressing themselves and their concerns, or are inhibited when talking to those with greater authority, power, or status, such as a boss or teacher. Conversely, the use of a minimal response may not be helpful when a speaker is not sufficiently motivated or eager to talk, or may need more extensive forms of feedback as in "active" listening, or more support and reassurance as in empathic listening.

Overlap or Interruption?

The use of minimal listening responses to enhance the flow of a conversation is one thing; having all the participants in a conversation enthusiastic and eager to speak is another. When everyone tries to talk at once it is at odds with the common view that conversation is an activity in which one person speaks at a time, an idea more suited to public than private communication. Apparently, most Americans believe one speaker *ought* to speak at a time, though this is seldom what actually occurs. In actual practice, Deborah Tannen found that informal conversation is characterized by overlaps—two or more voices sounding at once.[3] Generally, the overlap reflects a mutual, animated involvement and spontaneous expression with the primary aim of keeping the conversation lively. By contrast, silence often implies disinterest or boredom. Occasionally, people may engage in overlaps to an extreme degree, such as when they become excited or emotionally aroused about something. An example would be a television panel show in which several people begin speaking at once, with the idea that it is better to err on the side of enthusiasm than restraint. This may be stimulating, but it can also be confusing; it is rarely good communication.

Individuals differ in their acceptance and use of these conversational overlaps, probably, again, depending on many factors, such as differences in personality, geographical regions, expressiveness, cultures, and gender. For instance, individuals with a high involvement style tend to converse with enthusiasm, thereby creating many overlaps and expecting others to do so. Nor do they interpret such overlaps as interruptions. On the other hand, individuals who prefer a greater latitude of consideration tend to use and expect longer pauses between remarks. Consequently, they are more likely to construe an overlap as an interruption. Such differences may reflect regional differences, e.g., many New Yorkers and Californians use shorter pauses than those from the Midwest or New England. Thus, the frequency and interpretation of overlaps depends partly on the clash of various conversational styles.

By the same token, it is important to note that an overlap is not necessarily an interruption. Much depends on the impact or effect of the simultaneous occurrence of speech. For instance, women tend to engage in more overlaps than men, yet the overall impact of these overlaps is generally to increase the flow of conversation. While women are especially apt to use enhancing responses such as "mm-hm" and "yeah" as well as to ask questions and give feedback, they are also more apt to use retrieval responses, i.e, attempts to resume the line of communication from the point where the overlap occurred. Thus, in many instances overlaps may be an inherent part of good communication rather than genuine interruptions.

Consider this lively meeting between two friends who have not seen each other in a long time:

MARIE: Oh Joan, hi!

JOAN: —I can't believe my eyes! Marie? *(overlap)*

MARIE: —Where on earth have you been? *(overlap)*

JOAN: —Whatever are you doing here? *(overlap)*

MARIE: —It's great to see you! How's Chris? *(overlap)*

Both women talk at once but no information is exchanged until the joy and surprise die down. These are nondisruptive overlaps.

By contrast, men make fewer listener responses, but get accused of making more interruptions. In fact, one of the most widely cited findings is that men tend to interrupt women more than vice versa.[4] The reason for this may have more to do with the impact of their responses than their frequency. That is, in the course of listening, men are more apt to make challenging statements and initiate a change of subject. The net effect of the latter, especially, is to disrupt the flow of conversation, at least from the speaker's point of view. The tendency of a listener to switch the topic of conversation may stem from men's preference for the dominant role over a more cooperative role. Whether an overlap is seen as an interruption depends largely on the impact of the response on the flow of the conversation. Does it facilitate the flow, especially as initiated by the first speaker, or does it have the effect of switching the topic away from that initially expressed by the speaker? Interruptions disrupt the flow. Let's suppose Bob and Jack are setting up a sales demonstration together:

JACK: How about these paper samples? Some class!

BOB: Yeah, they're good. Where shall we put them?

JACK: —And these pricy covers—wow! *(interruption)*

BOB: Where do these papers go, Jack?

JACK: —These ought to bring 'em in! *(interruption)*

BOB: Hell, I'll stack them here.

Each man is on his own track. Because of Jack's enthusiastic interruptions there is no real communication.

Of course, when two people stick to the subject of their conversation, then mutually agree to move on to something else, this point becomes irrelevant.

The Use of Questions

Another type of listener response that may facilitate or impede the flow of conversation is the use of questions—at least the appropriate type of question. Open-ended questions such as "How do you feel about that?" may be especially helpful. This type of question requires more than a minimal one-word answer by the speaker. It is generally introduced with *what, where, when, who,* or *how.* The choice of the opening word is important, since each word tends to elicit different kinds of responses from speakers. *What* responses solicit facts and information. *Where* and *when* responses elicit specific information about time and place. *How* responses are used to inquire about emotions or sequences of events. *Who* questions elicit information about people. It is important to vary the words used to start open-ended questions, depending on the type of material you want to focus on and solicit from the speaker. For instance, if a friend or client wants to tell you about a problem in getting good service from a company, you might ask:

- ☐ What happens to make you feel dissatisfied?
- ☐ When do you notice this?
- ☐ How do things go wrong?
- ☐ Who is involved in this?

You may notice that the word *why* has been omitted as an appropriate opening word. This is because *why* questions seek reasons and motives, and often have an accusatory ring to them, putting speakers off and making them feel defensive. Yet, strangely enough, *why* questions frequently surface in conversations and interviews, usually with a disruptive effect. Consequently, I've initiated a simple technique in the classroom to increase awareness of the use of such questions. Whenever a listener asks "why?" of the speaker, all the other participants spontaneously clap their hands loudly, preferably in unison. This inevitably startles the listener who has made the offending response. In turn, the listener, and others vicariously, will tend to use *why* questions less frequently. As a helpful side effect, my own sensitivity to the use of *why* questions during teaching and conversations has been increased. Whenever I catch myself asking a rhetorical *why* in a lecture, I wince, and begin to rephrase my thoughts with a more suitable *what, when,* or *how* question.

Closed questions—those answered by *yes* or *no*—are not generally desirable when our primary purpose is to encourage the speaker to talk. However, when you want or need a specific piece of information, this can be the most suitable response. Even then, you should be aware that such questions narrow the focus of the conversation and restrict the speaker's input. Accordingly, closed-end questions should be used sparingly. Too many closed-end questions can discourage speaker expression, with the listener assuming too much control of the conversation. In fact, this is the major hazard of questioning, as it switches control from the initial speaker.

Conversation need not be a contest to see who speaks the most, nor should one person do all the listening. Instead, it's best when all partners alternate the speaking and listening roles in a way that makes for a mutually satisfying conversation. Also, as listeners, we can enhance the flow of conversation through animated listening, without needlessly interrupting or switching the subject. At the same time, it helps to realize that our partners often have different conversational styles from our own, depending on how they have learned to listen and to express themselves. We need to see these styles for what they are, without blaming people's personalities or questioning their motives or intentions. By becoming aware of the characteristic ways we talk and listen in conversations and determining how effective they are, we can then modify our habitual styles when they are not serving us well.

5

"Active" Listening Skills

The competent listener shares responsibility for communication, whether in conversation or other exchanges. An important way of achieving this is through "active" listening. Essentially, active listening is the process of giving nonjudgmental feedback to the speaker as a way of checking the accuracy of what has been heard. The adjective "active" implies that the listener goes beyond the inherent act of listening itself to actively verbalize his or her understanding of the speaker's message. This extra effort makes active listening riskier than more casual listening by expressing the listener's understanding openly and asking for the speaker's confirmation or correction. But more importantly, by doing this, the listener may achieve greater accuracy in understanding what is said.

The need of "active" listening arises from the all too frequent misunderstanding that occurs in everyday communication. For instance, while shopping together in a mall, my wife said, "I'll meet you at the main entrance in fifteen minutes." "Okay," I said, as we headed in different directions. About ten minutes later, as I prepared to walk toward the main entrance, I thought to myself, "Actually, there are two 'main' entrances. I wonder which one she meant." Taking a chance, I walked toward the entrance nearest the store I had just visited. When my wife failed to appear at the appointed time, I walked toward the entrance at the opposite end of the mall. When I met my wife I said, "I thought you meant the main entrance near the store I went shopping in." "No," she replied, "I meant the one we entered when we came into the mall." In retrospect, I realize that a simple clarification at the outset would have avoided the misunderstanding.

"Active" listening skills are necessary because of the difficulties inherent in the process of communication itself. Let's take a look at several of these.

First, most words have more than one meaning. There are over 14,000 different meanings for the 500 most commonly used words in the English language. This comes to about twenty-eight meanings per word. As you can readily see, this makes it difficult to determine what someone means by a given word without knowing its particular connotation to the speaker. Consequently, when you're uncertain what a person means by a given word or phrase, it's best to clarify this with the speaker. Most likely, the speaker will try to explain his or her meaning in different words. Of course, some individuals have difficulty expressing themselves in words, or choosing the most suitable word to express their intended meaning. Then too, all of us have trouble finding the right word to express our deeper emotions.

Second, messages must be decoded for their intended meaning. Just as the military establishment and secret service conceal its messages in codes for reasons of national security, so too, do individuals express their messages in codes for reasons of personal security. Even though we may be clear about what we're communicating ourselves, we tend to express or "code" these meanings in socially acceptable ways. We may choose our words carefully, or be subtle, or indirect, yet, by doing so, we often fail to convey the intended meaning in a way that the listener will readily understand. Consequently, listeners must provide the speaker feedback in order to decode the message properly. For instance, in order to avoid appearing authoritarian, bosses may "suggest" rather than "order" a worker to do something. So when the boss says "I'd like that job finished as soon as you can," the worker may interpret that to mean, "Get to it as soon as you finish your other jobs," which is even more removed from the boss's intended message, "Do it now." Of course, a more alert boss might send a message that is easier to understand, or a worker who actively listens would clarify what the boss means by asking "How soon do you want it?" thereby avoiding costly misunderstanding.

Third, listen to the person as well as to the message. This is because we transmit messages whose meanings are only partly apparent in the words themselves. The meanings lie largely within the person who sends the message. Such personal meanings are an expression of the whole person to some extent, not simply that person's thoughts and words, but also his or her attitudes, feelings, motives, and values. This is not to deny that the meanings of some messages are more apparent than others, especially those containing factual information. But the more personal meanings express deeper aspects of a speaker's personality, the more difficult it is to translate meaning adequately into words. We also listen to those messages through our own personal "filters," as described earlier. As you may recall, these include our attitudes, beliefs, expectations, memories, past experiences, and the like. As a result, we interpret and attribute meaning to people's messages partly on the basis of our own experience and partly by what is expressed. Hence there is a double need to actively listen as a way of checking the *understood* meaning with the speaker's *intended* meaning.

"Active" listening generally consists of several kinds of listening responses, including clarification, paraphrase, and summarization. Reflection, still another "active" listening response, pertains to the affective part of people's messages and will be covered under empathic listening in the next chapter. We will discuss the various "active" listening skills separately for instructional purposes, though in practice they are used in combination.

Clarifying

Clarifying responses ask the speaker to elaborate on an ambiguous or implied statement. Since most messages are expressed from an internal frame of reference, the meaning may not be readily apparent to others. Messages that are ambiguous or confusing need clarification. Thus, clarifying responses serve two purposes: *first,* to make the meaning of the speaker's message more explicit, and *second,* to confirm the accuracy of what has been heard.

To help you formulate a clarifying response, you might use the four-step strategy suggested by William and Sherilyn Cormier.[1]

1. What has this person told me?
2. Are there any vague and confusing parts of the message? If so, what are they?
3. How can I express this so that the speaker will clarify it?
4. Listen and observe to see how useful my clarification response is.

Let's see how this works in practice. Suppose you're a manager and someone in your division has made an appointment to see you. Shortly after being seated, the person says, "I just can't take it anymore around here." All too often, the manager charges ahead with a response without stopping to check on what the person meant. The listener (manager) invariably makes assumptions and draws conclusions that are distorted or premature. As a trained listener, you decide to apply the four steps.

WORKER: "I just can't take it anymore around here."

MANAGER:
   1. What has this person told me? That he can't take it anymore (asked and answered covertly).

    2. Are there any vague or confusing parts of his message? Yes. I'm not sure what he means by "can't take it anymore."

    3. Now, can I phrase a clarifying response? Let's try,

MANAGER: "Tell me what you mean by 'can't take it' anymore. I'm not sure what you mean by this phrase."

WORKER: "Well, I feel that my workload is too heavy. I always feel behind. I'm trying to do too much."

    4. Is the clarifying response effective? Yes because the worker explains more explicitly about his unhappiness at work.

Clarifying responses often begin with simple declarative statements or open-ended questions such as "Are you saying that . . ." (plus a rephrasing of the person's message). Generally, it's best to phrase clarifying responses in your own words that seem suitable to the speaker and occasion. While there is no one right way to phrase clarifying responses, the following "openers" may be useful:

☐ Would you say that again?
☐ I don't understand what you mean.
☐ Would you please clarify that?
☐ I don't get it.
☐ What do you mean by that?
☐ Would you translate that?

Such responses tell the speaker that you do not fully understand what is being said. Sometimes that is all that is needed because speakers often fail to realize they are not making themselves clear. A simple reminder may encourage the speaker to make a greater effort at making his or her message more explicit. Also, you'll focus your clarifying responses on the speaker's message or the process of communication itself, rather than on the speaker's personality or motives. By so doing, you encourage the speaker to *do* something, to communicate more clearly. If you were to imply that something might be wrong with the speaker, you'd put that person on the defensive, making it more difficult for him or her to clarify the message.

You will also note that several clarifying responses are "open" questions. That is, they serve as a stimulus for the speakers to enlarge or elaborate on their initial message. You can also use "closed" questions, which call for a simple yes or no response. Examples would be "Is that all you wanted to say?" and "Would you like help?" or "Would you prefer to do that yourself?" Yet, closed questions should be used sparingly for several reasons. First, they tend to disrupt the speaker's train of thought and the flow of conversation. Second, such questions quickly switch the focus of communication from the initial speaker to the listener, who then gains control of the conversation, quickly putting the speaker on the defensive. Consequently, open-end questions are usually preferable.

Paraphrasing

Paraphrasing consists of restating the gist of the speaker's message in the listener's own words as a way of checking on the accuracy of what has been heard. When you are unclear about what the speaker has said, you ask for clarification. When you think you understand what the speaker has said, it's more appropriate to paraphrase the message.

Use of the paraphrase may serve several purposes. First, a paraphrasing response tells the speaker you understand what has been said. If this is correct, the speaker can elaborate further. If not, the speaker may expand or clarify. Second, the paraphrasing response may help the speaker focus on a particular idea or aspect of his or her message that may be of special interest to the listener. Still another use of the paraphrase is to emphasize the main aspects of a problem when either the speaker or listener must reach a decision about it.

In creating a paraphrasing response, you might follow the

four-step strategy described earlier.[2] Let's suppose you are talking with your partner or spouse, who says, "I wish we went out more often, but I'm not sure we can afford to."

1. What has the speaker (my partner) told me? That she wants to go out more often, but she isn't certain we have the money.

2. What is the content (person, idea, or situation) of this message? What is she trying to tell me? She's bored staying at home. She wants us to have more of a social life, yet, she doesn't want it to create a financial hardship for us.

3. How can I restate the main message and rephrase this? "In other words, if we can *afford* it, you'd like us to have more of a social life?"

4. Listen and see if the speaker confirms your response. "Definitely."

When paraphrasing, keep in mind several key points: First, it is very important to paraphrase in your *own words*. Otherwise, you'll be "parroting" the speaker's message or words. When this occurs, the speaker is apt to respond with a minimal answer such as "That's right" or "I agree," thereby cutting the communication short. Or, the speaker may be put off by such a simplistic or obvious mimicking response. Typical paraphrasing responses often begin with phrases like:

- As I understand you . . .
- You mean . . .
- What I hear you saying . . .
- From your point of view . . .
- You think . . .
- Correct me if I'm wrong, but . . .
- In other words, . . .

Second, in paraphrasing you should be *selective* rather than try to capture an exhaustive repetition of what has been said. That is, you want to emphasize key ideas or phrases that will lead to further discussion or more complete understanding. Of course, in doing this you risk missing the main point. But this is precisely what paraphrasing is all about, expressing your understanding of the speaker's message in order to check on its accuracy. Third, paraphrasing usually focuses on the content of the message, rather than the feelings expressed. The latter are usually dealt with by reflecting feelings, a related "active" listening response discussed in the next chapter. In paraphrasing, we are primarily concerned with cognitive meanings and ideas, that is, understanding the spoken message.

Summarizing

Summarizing responses sum up the main ideas and feelings expressed by the speaker or speakers in the conversation up to that point. This is an important, but demanding skill because it requires the listener to be aware of the many things that have been discussed over time. Summarizing is especially appropriate for lengthy conversations and group meetings in which many issues have been covered.

Summarizing may serve several purposes. It may tie together different, sometimes fragmentary elements of the conversation or discussion, identifying a common theme or pattern that becomes apparent over time, say after several responses in this conversation or even later conversations. A helpful clue here is what I call "repeated themes," i.e., subjects or issues the speaker explicitly refers to several times in a conversation, often because they have not been heard or addressed.

Occasionally, summarizing responses serve to modify the pace or focus the direction of the conversation. For instance, after a lengthy digression or storytelling in a conversation or meeting, the listener might bring the conversation back to the point of digression by saying something like, "Now up to this point, we've discussed . . ." thereby getting the conversation back on track.

One of the most valuable purposes of summary re.
is to review what has been covered in a conversati
meeting. This may help speakers and listeners alike k
what has been communicated. Otherwise, the listeners n ..y
walk away from a conversation or meeting unsure if they've
heard the speaker's message. And the speaker, in turn, may
be uncertain whether his or her message has been heard.

For summarizing responses, too, you can apply the same
four-step strategy described earlier.[3] Let's say you're the
leader of a group planning a seminar or workshop on practical
things citizens can do to protect the environment in their
local community. After an hour and a half, toward the end of
your meeting, you ask yourself:

1. *What have we talked about so far?* We've talked about
a lot of different things we could do in the workshop, some
more practical than others.

2. *Are there any apparent themes or patterns? Is there
anything that keeps resurfacing in the discussion?* I keep
hearing a concern about which practices are more urgent or
needed at this point, as well as which ones are the most
practical.

3. *How can I sum up the patterns or themes of our
conversation?* (Remember to use paraphrasing or declarative
statements rather than a question.) Up to this point, we've
discussed a lot of interesting options. Now I think we have to
decide which ones we're most interested in pursuing and
make our plans accordingly.

4. *Now listen and see if others confirm my summary
response or not.* Observe whether there is a reasonable
consensus in responses to my statement.

As with the other "active" listening responses described so
far, it's best to put summary statements into your own words.
It's also preferable to use declarative statements rather than
questions. Here are some typical prefaces for summary statements:

- ☐ What we have said so far is . . .
- ☐ Your main suggestions, as I get them, are . . .
- ☐ Everything we have discussed so far . . .
- ☐ Now, summing up . . .
- ☐ Recapping what you have said . . .
- ☐ So far, we have talked about these options . . .

Summarizing responses may be useful at the close of a telephone conversation, especially when several key points have been covered, or something is to be done by the speaker or the listener. Summarizing is especially appropriate in situations that involve a discussion of differences, complaints, conflicts, or problem-solving. It is generally helpful in group meetings in which the prolonged discussion of a subject or subjects may become complicated, if not confusing. Without summary statements, the group may spend its energy reacting to surface manifestations of a problem rather than the basic issues, and members go away uncertain as to what, if anything, was accomplished in the meeting.

I once belonged to an executive committee of an organization that met one evening each month. Generally, we covered a wide range of subjects, from finances to promotion. But probably the only person who kept track of all the business was the person who took the minutes of the meeting. This usually became evident at future meetings, when the individuals responsible for implementing the various decisions had not carried out their responsibilities. Then one member, who was a retired executive, suggested that the secretary of the committee summarize the group's actions that evening, along with a reminder of who was responsible for carrying out which decisions. This way, everyone left the meeting with a better awareness of what we had accomplished, along with a clearer idea of what each person was responsible for.

6

Empathic Listening

Empathic listening means experiencing another person's inner world as if stepping into the speaker's own shoes. An empathic listener seeks to gain an accurate understanding of the other person from his or her own personal frame of reference, and to convey that understanding back to the person. Such understanding, however, involves more than the use of listening techniques, as valuable as these are. Empathic listening and understanding also depend on our attitudes and relationships to others, and are therefore very demanding. Even experienced therapists who aspire to empathic listening generally fall short of the ideal in actual practice.

If empathic listening is so difficult to achieve, why try? You will be in a better position to answer that after reading this chapter. Meanwhile, consider this: Empathy is probably *the* most potent factor in building rapport with people, in achieving an accurate understanding of their thoughts and feelings, and in eliciting their cooperation both as individuals and in groups.[1]

The need for empathic listening can be seen in the egocentric indifference to others that has become so prevalent in everyday life. In our efforts at personal survival as well as in the pursuit of fulfillment, we tend to give top priority to our own needs. Yet, in so doing we jeopardize our relationships with others, an equally indispensable part of human fulfillment. By contrast, the need for empathy reminds us that we must strike a better balance between the claims of self and others. Empathy tends to humanize and socialize us, encouraging us to reach out to people and to form more mutually satisfying relationships with them. Individuals completely lacking in empathy, like the antisocial personality, remain overly preoccupied with the gratification of their own needs in ways that make them callous. Such individuals are characterized by *apathy* (without feeling), lacking the normal feelings and concerns for others. Not far behind are the narcissistic personalities—thought by some to be the characteristic disorder of our time—who are so wrapped up in themselves that they are incapable of empathy or closeness.

At the opposite extreme, people who become overly *sympathetic* (feeling "for" another) tend to become overinvolved and overidentified with others. This in turn leads to an uncritical acceptance of and dependence on others and their problems, thereby jeopardizing their own survival as well as compounding the problems of others. Most of us probably fall somewhere in between these two extremes, attempting to balance self-interest with the concern for others in varying degrees. We might call ourselves "realistic," though in practice, if the truth were known, we run the risk of having too little, rather than too much empathy. Learning to listen empathically will help us to develop our natural human tendency toward empathy.

Empathy

Empathy (feeling "with" or "into" another) may be defined as the ability to understand another person from his or her own internal frame of reference. Empathy implies that we attempt to think and feel "with," rather than "for" or "about" the person.[2] To empathize is to become sensitive to someone's innermost feelings, perceptions, intentions, and felt meanings, and then to convey this understanding back to the person for his or her confirmation. It means frequently checking with the person for the accuracy of your perceptions and being guided in turn by their responses. Accordingly, empathy is more a process than a condition or state of being. In everyday language, empathy is often expressed as "getting inside another person," "viewing the world through another's eyes," listening to others with "ears like theirs," and "walking in someone else's shoes." An age-old proverb says "Never judge anyone until you have stood in that person's shoes for a whole day."

It's important to realize that empathy involves the accurate understanding of someone else *as if* we were the person, without ever losing the "as if" condition. Thus, empathy isn't some mystical union or fusion with another person in which the listener loses his or her self. As empathic listeners we retain our personal identities, at the same time temporarily setting aside our critical judgment and prejudices for the sake of more fully understanding the other person from his or her own frame of reference. In fact, it is our own capacity to experience the same meanings others do that enables us to understand them empathically. That is, we *infer* or imagine what it must be like for others on the basis of our own personal experience.

To be effective, empathy must be *expressed* and *perceived* by the other person, who in this instance is the speaker. Although it is now thought that most people have the potential for empathy, individuals differ in their ability to experience and express it, largely because of the way they are socialized. For instance, children who are disciplined harshly or abused by their parents tend to be low in empathy. On the other hand, children who receive a great deal of affection from their parents tend to be high in empathy. Then too, women are often described as more sensitive to the feelings of others than men are. Yet, when researchers look at people's abilities to describe other people's feelings and respond to their problems, they don't find consistent differences between men and women.[3] There are apt to be greater differences between individuals, regardless of sex.

When it comes to empathic listening, there are three main

things a listener can do to convey empathy. First, show our desire to understand the person. Second, reflect the person's feelings or felt meanings. And third, pace the person's sensory and nonverbal behavior.[4] We'll explain each of these in that order.

Show Your Desire to Understand

Showing your *desire* to understand helps to maintain the relationship with the other person when your understanding falls short of the mark, as it often does. Generally, this involves the use of nonverbal as well as verbal responses. For instance, suppose you tell a person, "Go ahead, tell me how you feel about this project—I'm listening." Then you lean back in your chair and look disinterested or bored. Chances are the person will not be convinced you really *want* to understand. This is because whenever your behavior contradicts your words, people are more apt to believe your behavior.

Remember to make use of the attending skills described in chapter 3. That is, minimize possible distractions that keep you from giving the speaker your undivided attention. Concentrate on what the speaker is saying. When your mind wanders, deliberately bring your thoughts back to the speaker and what he or she is saying to you. Maintain appropriate eye contact with the speaker to show you're interested—alternately looking and looking away. Be an animated listener. Use minimal responses and open-ended questions that show the speaker you're involved. At the same time, it's important to adapt your listening to the person and immediate situation. For instance, high levels of attentiveness may be too intense for some people, especially during an initial contact.

Using "active" listening skills is a major way of indicating your desire to make sense of the person's inner world. Responding to a vague or ambiguous statement by asking for clarification, rather than simply letting it pass, shows you want to understand. Then too, paraphrasing the speaker's main points not only demonstrates you really do understand but also encourages the person to elaborate. Summarizing responses serve to tie together various aspects of a conversation or, at times, to review what has been covered, which is especially important when deciding on a particular course of action.

Another way of expressing your desire to understand someone is to discuss what is important to that person. If you must interrupt, show by your questions and comments that you are aware of what is important. Do not change the subject until the speaker indicates his or her readiness to do so. For instance, perhaps you have had the experience of changing the subject of a conversation, only to have the other person ignore your remarks and return to his or her original subject. Repeated attempts to retrieve the subject discussed earlier remind us to return to what is important to the speaker. Consequently, if and when we interrupt the speaker's flow of expression, we should attempt to follow with a retrieval response, i.e., go back to the speaker's earlier theme to encourage further discussion of what is most important.

Expressing your desire to understand others is especially crucial in those situations in which people are less likely to believe we want to understand, such as occasions of serious disagreement, conflicts, personal complaints, or situations involving intense emotions. At such times there is a tendency to take things personally, i.e., to equate disagreement over an issue with personal rejection. The more you try "talking" someone into accepting your views, the more defensive that person is likely to become. By contrast, showing your desire to listen is a major way of demonstrating that you care about the person, that you're open to communication. The willingness to listen first not only provides an opportunity to gain more understanding of the person's views, or where he or she is "coming from," but also increases the possibility that this person will extend the same courtesy to you.

Reflect the Person's Feelings

An old, eastern proverb goes "Listen to what people *say*, but find out how they *feel*." Accordingly, when we think we understand someone's feelings, acknowledging them is the next step in conveying our empathy. The most effective way to do this is by reflecting back to the speaker the feelings being expressed. The reflection response is similar in *form* to the paraphase in that it expresses back to the speaker what you understand the spoken message to be. But there is an important difference in the *content* of the response. The reflection focuses on the affective component of the message or feelings expressed, whereas the paraphrase focuses on the cognitive or verbal component. Consider the following example:

> **SPEAKER:** "Things are kind of dull right now. There's nothing new or exciting. It's just the same old schedule."

> **LISTENER PARAPHRASE:** You're just doing the same old routine things.

> **LISTENER REFLECTION:** You feel bored with an uninteresting situation.

Notice the listener's use of the affect word *bored* to emphasize the feelings being expressed.

Reflecting feelings may serve several purposes. First, when done correctly, it helps people to feel understood. Often what people are most intent on expressing are attitudes, felt meanings, or feelings about something. Second, reflection encourages people to become more aware of their feelings as well as to express those feelings. Some people do not readily disclose their feelings, either because they have never learned to do so or do not feel comfortable doing so. In either case, helping speakers to become more fully aware of their feelings about a particular issue may aid in their understanding and expression about it. Third, reflection helps speakers discriminate more accurately among various feelings. A speaker may say "I'm uptight" to express intense feelings of worry and panic. Accurate reflection helps the person to define his or her feelings. Finally, reflection is especially helpful in expressing negative feelings, such as anger, fear, and sadness. When people become upset with us, we have a tendency to take their remarks personally and become defensive. Reflecting their particular feelings by saying something such as "You feel sad right now" conveys more empathic understanding than simply saying, "I know how you feel." A reflection response helps people to express their feelings more fully, which, in turn, serves to diminish negative feelings and facilitate communication.

In reflecting feelings, you might find it helpful to use the four-step strategy suggested earlier.[5] For example, when asked, a man explains why he doesn't want to serve on your committee:

SPEAKER: "Most of the time it's an exercise in futility. You spend all that time coming up with various options and then people ignore your suggestions. It's too frustrating."

1. What feelings are being expressed by the speaker? Listen for the affect or feeling words in the person's messages. In this case, he feels frustrated, thwarted, and that it's all futile.

2. Watch for the nonverbal behavior accompanying the verbal message. Nonverbal behavior is often a more reliable clue to the feelings being expressed than the words used. This speaker is shaking his head, frowning, and tightening his lips.

3. Reflect the speaker's feelings back to him, using different words. For instance, if the speaker expressed feeling mixed up, interchangeable affect words would be "confused," "doubtful," and "unsure."

LISTENER: "You feel thwarted or unproductive serving on this type of committee."

4. Listen and observe the speaker's response to see how effective your reflection is.

SPEAKER: "You can say that again. I feel it's a waste of my time."

Since the purpose of reflecting feelings is to let the speaker know we understand how he or she feels, our responses should be phrased in our own words. To give an idea, here are some familiar opening phrases:

□ You feel . . .
□ Perhaps you are feeling . . .
□ Do you feel a little . . .
□ You are (angry, sad, etc.) . . .
□ I sense that you feel . . .
□ You are feeling a bit . . .

Responses that convey your awareness of the person's *explicit* feelings are often labeled "primary" empathy. This is the minimal response that conveys your awareness of the other person's frame of reference. In contrast, when a listener has a deeper comprehension of the person's innermost, unspoken thoughts and feelings, the response may refer implicitly to these. This is called "advanced" empathy.[6] Here, the listener is so much inside the private world of another person that he or she can clarify not only what the other person is clearly aware of, but also that which the person may be only dimly aware of, if at all, yet which is implied or inferred in what has been said. For instance, suppose a friend, who seeks you out as a sounding board, says, "I've tried to get along with my wife. But things just aren't working out for us." If you were to respond to the explicit feelings expressed, you might say, "You feel discouraged because your efforts to get along with your wife aren't succeeding." This would be the minimal type of response to convey empathy. However, if you are very familiar with this person's marital situation, you might pick up some of the deeper, more implied feelings being expressed. Here, you might say, "You feel discouraged because you can't seem to get along with your wife. You want her to become more cooperative. One thing you could do is to share your feelings about this with her." This would be an example of advanced empathy. Although the concept of primary and advanced empathy is helpful in understanding the full range of empathy, it is more pertinent to the work of the psychotherapist.

Pace the Person's Sensory and Nonverbal Behavior

Empathy is conveyed not only through verbal messages and reflecting feelings. It may also be expressed through attentive nonverbal behaviors. These nonverbal behaviors are especially useful when they pace or match the speaker's nonverbal behavior. Essentially, pacing means matching the speaker's nonverbal behavior without mimicking the person or doing it in such a deliberate manner that the speaker becomes aware of it.[7]

The importance of pacing the speaker's nonverbal behavior is based on the principle that people's words and behaviors not only reveal their ideas and feelings, but also how they process information and organize their experience. Much of the processing occurs through the various sensory channels. These are: visual (sight), auditory (hearing), kinesthetic (feeling), olfactory (smell), and gustatory (taste). The three major channels are seeing, hearing, and feeling. Each of us generally has a preference for a particular sensory channel or mode of experience that in turn, is used more often. Individuals reveal their use of these sensory channels by various nonverbal behaviors, such as eye movements and voice tone, as well as selected verbal behaviors. Studies have shown that listen-

ers who match a speaker's sensory systems by responding
with similar verbal and nonverbal behaviors are perceived as
more empathic.[8]

Individuals unwittingly disclose the sensory channel they
are using at the time by their language, especially the verbs,
adjectives, and adverbs. For instance, if a speaker says something like "I don't like what I see" or "from my point of view,"
the words *see* and *point of view* suggest that this person is
processing information visually. Here, the responsive listener
would match the speaker's mode of experiencing by using
words that evoke images and mental pictures, such as "As you
see it" or "the way you look at it." Similarly, a speaker who
uses words such as hearing, telling, and talking is processing
information in the auditory mode, involving an internal dialogue. Again, listeners who respond in the same sensory
mode tend to be perceived as more empathic. Also, the
person who uses such words as feel, touch, and experience is
relying primarily on the kinesthetic mode, by generating
visceral or internal sensations. Empathic listeners would respond in words such as "I sense that" or "I have the feeling
that . . ." In each case, listeners can identify the person's
sensory system by listening closely to the key words used and
responding in a similar way.

EXAMPLES OF SPEAKER'S SENSORY WORDS

VISUAL

look	bright	gaze
colorful	view	clear
picture	sight	watch
see	viewpoint	appears

AUDITORY

talk	overhear	shout
hear	say	tell

listen	sounds	tune
loud	quiet	deaf

KINESTHETIC

touch	soft	strain
relax	pain	grasp
sensing	hard	squeeze
feel	tense	clutch

Matching the person's momentary experience also involves the use of similar, nonverbal expressions. That is, the listener adjusts his or her nonverbal behavior to that of the speaker. However, it is very important to do this gracefully. Just as you do not simply parrot or mimic the words in paraphrasing and reflecting responses, you do not directly mirror the person's body language. Instead, matching nonverbal behaviors should occur naturally and subtly, just enough to make the person feel he or she is being understood.

Consider the following ways you can match someone's nonverbal behavior:

☐ *Facial expressions:* Observe how the face is used, e.g., raising of eyebrows, widening or narrowing of eyes, frowning, pursing of lips, etc.

☐ *Posture:* Adjust your stance to mirror the other person's posture, such as standing with arms on the hips or sitting in a relaxed fashion.

☐ *Gestures:* Use some of the person's characteristic gestures, such as repeated hand motions.

☐ *Voice:* Adjust the tone, tempo, and volume of your voice to more nearly match that of your partner.

Matching is especially important in the initial stages of a relationship when you are establishing rapport. Matching does not mean giving up your own way of processing experience or expressing yourself. Mainly, it can be used selectively in understanding your speaker and building rapport. You might practice with your friends as a way of using this skill without losing sight of the larger task of listening and understanding. Matching the person's mode of experience and nonverbal behavior can be a powerful aid in conveying that you and your partner are "speaking the same language."

To recap briefly, when you want to listen empathically: show you want to understand, reflect the person's feelings, and pace that person's sensory and nonverbal behavior. When people feel deeply understood they are more apt to feel accepted, cared for, and valued by the listener. Much of the effect of empathic understanding comes from the nonjudgmental quality of listening. That is, people feel they have been given an opportunity to express themselves in their own words and thus to be accurately understood. In turn, they feel freer to elaborate on their own thoughts, feelings, and attitudes. Thus, empathy elicits more information and disclosure from people than would be extracted by probing questions. Lastly, empathy enhances cooperation and builds rapport with individuals in both one-to-one relationships and groups.

7

Nonverbal Communication

Our awareness of nonverbal communication is reflected in many of our popular figures of speech. We speak of happy people being "filled with joy" or "bursting with pride." We see fearful people as "paralyzed" or "frozen" with fear. Angry people may be described as "trembling with rage," "bursting at the seams," or "ready to explode." Tense people are portrayed as "biting their lips." In each of these examples, people are expressing their feelings through their bodies as well as their words. While experts differ in their estimates, it is safe to say that more than half of our face-to-face communication is nonverbal. Listening to the speaker's message, then, means learning how to read his or her body language as well and responding appropriately.

Reading Body Language
Essentially, nonverbal communication, popularly known as "body language," includes all those behavioral expressions that do not rely on words or word symbols.

Learning how to read these bodily expressions is important for several reasons. First, while words may readily convey factual knowledge, words alone are rarely adequate to express our feelings. Sometimes we say "I am not sure how to express this in words," meaning our feelings are more intense or somewhat more complex than we can find words for. Yet these unverbalized feelings are inevitably expressed in nonverbal behavior. Second, our body language also shows how we are coping with those feelings. If a speaker is having difficulty controlling her anger, she might raise her voice, turn away, or become physically aggressive. Third, body language tells us how people feel about us. A speaker who points, glares, or makes constant interruptions is conveying an entirely different feeling toward us than one who smiles and is relaxed and listens to us. Finally, nonverbal communication is especially valuable in that it tends to be unintentional or unconscious. That is, even though people measure their words, and attempt to control their facial expressions, there is often a "leakage" of masked feelings, perhaps in their gaze, gestures, or tone of voice. Any of these nonverbal expressions may help us to confirm what is said verbally, or sometimes question it.

Two words of caution are in order. First, popular knowledge has it that nonverbal expressions have universal meaning, for example, folded arms always mean defensiveness. This simply isn't true. Instead, specific nonverbal expressions like folded arms are best understood in relation to the particular situation in which they occur. For example, I once saw a hypnotist performer ask for volunteers to come onto the stage for a demonstration of hypnosis. Among all those who raised their hands to volunteer, I noticed he selected only those who were sitting in a relaxed posture, with arms open, some even slouched down in their seats. He did not take anyone with crossed arms or legs. In both cases, he had read their body language to indicate their attitude toward hypnosis. I doubt that the hypnotist would have made the mistake of thinking all people with folded arms or crossed legs were generally overinhibited, neurotic people. Rather, he probably realized the first rule of understanding nonverbal communication— namely, that body language must be read in the context of the situation.

The other caution concerns not situational but cultural differences. Author Julius Fast tells of a fifteen-year-old Puerto Rican girl who had been caught in the washroom with a group of girls suspected of smoking.[1] Although most of the others were known troublemakers, Livia had no record of trouble. Yet, after being interviewed by the principal she was presumed to be guilty. The principal referred to her suspicious attitude, expressed in not looking him in the eye. He took this as a sign of guilt. The incident led to protests of the mother and a demonstration of Puerto Rican parents at school the next morning. Fortunately, a Spanish teacher at the school, who knew Livia, told the principal that in Puerto Rico nice girls do not look directly at adults, as a sign of respect and obedience. The principal had misread Livia's nonverbal behavior. Perhaps the incident added an important item to his body language "vocabulary" so that he would no longer confuse shyness with guilt.

Ordinarily, we achieve a more accurate understanding of a person's body language when we view it in relation to the particular situation as well as the person's social and cultural background. At the same time, some people are better than others in reading body language. Several studies have shown that women are more accurate both in sending and receiving nonverbal messages of emotion. Yet male psychiatrists, psychologists, and teachers, as well as actors, artists, and designers score as high as women.[2] That is, decoding body language is largely a learned ability. Then too, individuals of both sexes vary widely among themselves, with some people being good senders but poor receivers, and others just the opposite. Generally, our sensitivity to nonverbal messages increases with age and experience. How about yourself? Would you say you are getting better at reading body language? I hope the following pages will help you to gain a greater awareness of the meaning and importance of nonverbal expressions.

Facial Expressions

Facial expressions are the major indicators of emotions. Positive emotions such as happiness, love, and surprise are the easiest to recognize. Negative emotions such as sadness,

anger, and disgust are usually the most difficult to recognize.
The following facial expressions are often associated with
these six basic emotions:

- ☐ Surprise: lifted eyebrows, wide-open eyes, dropped-open
  mouth, parted lips.
- ☐ Fear: eyebrows raised and drawn together, eyes opened
  wide, corners of the mouth drawn back, lips stretched,
  mouth may or may not be open.
- ☐ Anger: eyebrows furrowed, sometimes curved forehead
  wrinkles, eyes squinting, lips pressed together or bared
  teeth.
- ☐ Disgust: lowered eyebrows, wrinkled nose, mouth open,
  forward lower lip or mouth closed with upper lip pushed up
  by lower lip.
- ☐ Sadness: eyebrows drawn together, eyes glazed, with
  drooping upper lip, mouth either open or closed with outer
  corners pulled slightly down.
- ☐ Happiness: no distinctive eyebrows, relaxed eyes, outer
  corners of lips raised, usually drawn back.[3]

The mouth and lips are especially expressive of people's
feelings. We are all familiar with the pursed lips associated
with deep thought, or the smirking lips that often accompany
doubt or sarcasm. Smiling is mostly a social expression communicating a sense of pleasure, humor, friendliness, or the
need for approval. For some reason, women generally smile
more than men. At the same time, smiling behavior is also
affected by regional and cultural differences, with southerners
tending to smile more, while upstate New Yorkers and New
Englanders smile less than average. Since smiling reflects
more than one motive, we should be careful not to overinter-
pret a speaker's smiles. However, excessive smiling often
expresses a need for approval or deference to authority.

Because the face is so expressive of feelings, speakers often
attempt to control or "mask" their facial expressions. For

instance, when someone accidentally bumps into us or has made a mistake, he or she may feel as annoyed as we do, but smile instinctively as if to express a polite apology. In this case, the smile may be a bit "canned," or forced, betraying a mixture of annoyance and apology.

Gazing and Eye Contact

Since most of what we learn comes through our visual sense, we are twice as likely to look while listening than while speaking. Looking is an extremely important part of communication. It not only shows the speaker we are interested; it also helps us pay better attention to what is being said.

Interestingly, during a conversation both the speaker and the listener tend to adopt an alternate "look" and "look-away" pattern. It is as if constant looking would be too distracting to the speaker or to the listener's concentration. Both speaker and listener look at each other for anywhere from one to ten seconds. This is likely to occur immediately after the speaker says something. From time to time, the speaker's and listener's eyes will meet in eye contact, though these instances are usually of shorter duration than one-way gazing of either partner.

We are more apt to maintain eye contact with the speaker while discussing pleasant topics, like our plans for the coming weekend. On the other hand, we are more likely to avoid eye contact while discussing unpleasant or embarrassing topics, such as a mistake of either partner or the termination of the relationship. In the latter instance, avoidance of eye contact is an expression of politeness and consideration of the other's feelings. Excessive or inappropriate eye contact in times like these tends to be resented as an intrusion on one's privacy. Moreover, too much eye contact or staring is usually taken as a sign of hostility. The hostile significance of staring may be seen in the fact that animals usually stare at each other just before attacking.

We also need to be aware that looking reflects other aspects of the overall relationship. For instance, we tend to look more at those whom we admire or with whom we have a more intimate relationship. Also, women tend to have greater eye contact than men, probably because they feel more comfortable with intimacy. On the other hand, people avoid eye contact in competitive situations, lest this be construed as a sign of hostility. Futhermore, we tend to look more when we are at a distance from the speaker. The closer we get to the speaker, the more we avoid eye contact. Generally, eye contact helps speakers to feel they are communicating with us, and to have a more favorable impression of us, but excessive or inappropriate gazing, including constant eye contact, often gives others a negative impression of us.

Looking helps to regulate conversation in a couple of ways. First of all, initial eye contact helps us to catch the speaker's eye. We often speak of the need to "catch the waiter's eye." As long as the speaker is using the alternate looking-and-looking-away pattern, he or she probably hasn't finished speaking. When finished, a speaker tends to look directly at the listener as if to say "I am through, now it is your turn."

Vocal Expressions

A good listener "reads between the lines,"—hears more than the speaker's words. He also hears the speaker's pitch, tone of voice, and rate of speech. He notices the variations of speech, like failing to complete a sentence and/or pausing frequently. Next to the speaker's words and facial expressions, these vocal expressions are the most helpful clues to the speaker's message.

Tone of voice is an especially valuable clue to feelings. Rollo May, a famous psychotherapist, often asks himself "What does the voice say when I stop listening to the words and listen only to the tone?"[4] Feelings will be expressed regardless of the words that are spoken. People can accurately express their emotions even while reciting the alphabet! From the listener's standpoint, anger and sadness are usually the easiest to recognize, while nervousness and jealousy are among the most difficult.

The volume and pitch of the speaker's voice, how high or low, or how loud or soft it sounds, are also helpful in decoding the speaker's message. Some emotions like enthusiasm, joy, and disbelief are usually delivered in a high pitch. Anger and fear are also expressed in a high pitch, as well as in a wider range of tone and pitch of volume. On the other hand, apathy and emotions like sadness and grief are usually expressed softly and in a low pitch, especially toward the end of each sentence.

The rate of speech also tells us something about the speaker's feelings. People talk faster when they are excited or anxious, or when they are speaking about a personal problem or something that is threatening to them. People are also apt to speak faster when they are trying to persuade us or sell us something. On the other hand, people usually talk more slowly when they are depressed, grief-stricken, disgusted, contemptuous, or tired.

People unwittingly express their feelings and personalities through minor speech disturbances, such as repeating words, vacillating in their choice of words, or failing to complete a sentence. People tend to vacillate in choosing words when they are unsure of themselves or are getting ready to surprise us. Those who stutter often speak perfectly well until they become anxious, then lapse into stuttering. Generally these speech disturbances are more intrusive when the speaker is anxious or is trying to deceive us.

The listener should also be aware of meanings expressed in vocal variations such as a groan, grunt, sigh, nervous cough, tongue-clicking, raspberry, and so on. The variety is endless. Again, it is essential to realize that more meaning can usually be expressed in sounds rather than words. This is also true of the language of gestures.

Posture and Gestures

People reveal their attitudes and feelings by the way they stand or sit, and the way they move various parts of their bodies.

We take it as a compliment when speakers lean toward us in a conversation, probably because this posture suggests they are attentive. On the other hand, we feel less favorable toward those who lean away from us or slouch down in their chairs while speaking with us. Generally we feel more comfortable talking with someone who adopts a relaxed posture, although persons with a higher status than ours are more likely to adopt such a posture, probably because they feel more secure in the relationship. That is, they will sit rather than stand, or they will recline or lean sideways rather than sit erect.

The angle at which people feel comfortable sitting or standing in relation to each other varies with the nature of the situation, or with sex and culture differences. When people know each other well or are in a cooperative situation, they generally prefer to stand or sit at a right angle to one another. When they are meeting strangers or are in a bargaining situation, they feel more comfortable in a face-to-face position. Women often prefer to converse with their partners at a slight angle or side-by-side, especially if they know them well. Men often prefer the face-to-face position, unless they are in a competitive situation. People in the United States and England generally prefer to position themselves at a right angle to their partners, while Swedes tend to avoid this position. On the other hand, Arabs prefer the head-on position.[5] If you are unsure which position your partners feel most comfortable in, watch where they stand, sit, or move their chairs when given the freedom to do so.

Many gestures of the arms or legs are somewhat obvious in meaning. For instance, crossed arms or legs usually signal a somewhat skeptical, defensive attitude, whereas uncrossed limbs express a more open, trusting attitude. Cupping one's hands under the chin is a sign of a thoughtful attitude. Putting hands on the hips may signal defiance or readiness to begin a task. Folding the arms behind one's head is an expression of dominance toward others. People are constantly moving their heads throughout a conversation. While nodding the head does not always mean agreement, it does help the flow of conversation, as if giving the speaker permission to continue. Head nods also tend to reinforce the speaker, so that in a group speakers tend to speak more directly to those who consistently nod their heads. On the other hand, rapid nods or turning the head aside and gesturing with the hands often indicate to a speaker that a listener wishes to talk.

Generally, speakers and listeners alike prefer partners with animated facial expressions and expressive body movements. The frequent use of gestures on either person's part is taken as a sign of interest and friendliness, conveying positive feelings. An excessive use of gestures, however, may be an expression of anxiety or the lack of confidence in being able to communicate verbally.

Personal Space

How close or far apart people space themselves in relation to each other is another important factor in communication. Sometimes we even speak of relationships in spatial terms like "keeping our distance" from someone we dislike or fear, or "getting close" to someone we like. Generally, the more interested two people are in each other, the closer together they sit or stand. But there is a definite limit to how close people will let others come. Studies have shown that the distance between people in conversation, at least in the United States, depends largely on the type of interaction, as follows:

□ Intimate distance (within 18 inches)—This is appropriate for intimate behavior like lovemaking or wrestling, and is re- served for close friends or those in body contact sports.

- Personal distance (1½ to 4 feet)—for conversation between friends, with or without touching.
- Social distance (4 to 12 feet)—for informal social and business transactions, with more formal business transactions at the upper range.
- Public distance (12 feet and beyond)—At this distance we tend to acknowledge others with a minimum of speaking, preferring nonverbal gestures.[6]

Generally, people feel more comfortable and form a more favorable impression of someone when they stand or sit within the appropriate distance for a given type of transaction. Getting too close or remaining too distant affects communication negatively. Also, the closer people get, the less they look at each other, as if to respect each other's privacy, and the further away they get, the more they look and use gestures while talking, as if to insure keeping the other's attention.

These rules vary considerably depending on other factors such as age, sex, and culture. For instance, children and old people prefer to come closer, while adolescents and middle-aged people prefer more distance. Generally, women prefer standing or sitting closer to someone of either sex than men do, probably because women are more comfortable with intimate relationships. Personality is another factor, with people with high self-esteem coming closer, while more anxious people keep further away. Status and power also affect the distance between people. We generally prefer greater distance between ourselves and those with higher status and power than us, while people of equal status come closer together. Culture is another factor. People from Latin America and Mediterranean countries tend to come closer to their partners in conversation, while people from Northern European countries like the Swedes, Scots, and English keep more distant. Americans fall somewhere in between.[7]

Desks may also structure the distance between people

when they are talking. A desk is generally associated with a position of authority, so that when a listener sits behind a desk it is likely to be more of a role transaction. While this may afford a sense of relief to some partners, it tends to inhibit others. For this reason, some administrators and executives prefer holding interviews and personal conferences in a conversation corner away from their desks, with two chairs positioned at an angle to each other.

Responding to Nonverbal Communication

Interestingly, one way we respond to a speaker's nonverbal communication is by unconsciously copying his or her posture and facial expressions. That is, when a speaker folds her arms or crosses her legs, we may find ourselves automatically adopting the same gestures. It may be that we are responding to the speaker with bodily empathy, as if to say "I am with you. Go ahead."

Verbally responding to a speaker's nonverbal communication is another matter. Ordinarily, we should respond to the speaker's nonverbal expressions in relation to his or her overall communication. That is, when a speaker's facial expressions, tone of voice, and posture are consistent with his or her words, there is no problem. Here, the bodily expressions help to drive home the spoken word, so that we are more certain to "get the message." When the nonverbal expressions conflict with the speaker's words, however, we tend to favor the former. As the popular saying goes, "Actions speak louder than words."

When there are minor discrepancies between a speaker's words and body language, as when someone hesitates several times in inviting us to something, we may or may not choose to respond verbally to these conflicting nonverbal expressions. A lot depends on the people involved, the nature of their relationship, and the particular situation. But we rarely ignore these nonverbal expressions. Instead, conflicting body signals often lead us to delay action on a request or to have second thoughts after the conversation is ended. In other words, the nonverbal tends to register with us, often with a lag in time. Consequently, when we are getting "mixed signals" from a speaker, we may choose to say something like "I will think it over" or "I will get back to you on this," giving us time to evaluate the speaker's overall communication before making a firm decision.

When there are marked discrepancies between a speaker's words and nonverbal signals, a verbal expression to the mixed message may be in order. Perhaps the most skillful example of this comes from Dr. Fritz Perls's practice of Gestalt therapy, in which he deliberately observes and responds to the patient's nonverbal expressions as an integral part of bringing about therapeutic self-understanding. For example, in one training film, Dr. Perls called attention to a female patient's fidgeting with her hands, squirming in her seat, and nervously smiling and giggling. He pointed out that such behavior masked her feelings of dependency and her attempts to manipulate him to give her the answers. Even though the patient initially responded in a defensive manner, she eventually became more aware of her feelings and manipulative behavior with authority figures.

Ordinarily, it is advisable to respond to a speaker's conflicting nonverbal expressions with much greater tact. For example, if a speaker has agreed to do something for you, but is giving off mixed signals of doubt, such as frequent pauses, questions, or puzzled facial expressions, you may choose to respond to the latter by saying something like "You seem a bit skeptical about this. Would you like to talk about it?" Such a tactful response shows that you are attentive to the speaker's overall communication, yet careful not to arouse that person's anxiety and defensiveness. It simply provides the speaker with an opportunity to express himself or herself more fully.

To summarize, the art of listening effectively depends on

more than an accurate comprehension of the speaker's words. Communication also includes nonverbal signals which may confirm, or sometimes negate, the spoken message. Being sensitive to these nonverbal meanings will help listeners make the right interpretations and responses for more efficient and satisfying overall communication.

8

Attitude Is All-Important

When we are starting to improve our listening habits we may become preoccupied with the techniques of listening at the expense of the proper attitude for listening. This is especially true in the early stages of retraining our listening habits, when we may come across as awkard or phony, or not ourselves. Even beginning counselors and therapists sometimes fall into this trap. Therefore, those who train professional therapists warn of confusing the accepting and empathic attitude, so essential for listening, with a "wooden technique" of simply repeating everything a person says, which would be a perversion of listening. Hence a separate chapter is devoted to attitudes.

Attitudes are beliefs and feelings that predispose us to act in certain ways toward people, objects, and events. Rarely are we completely neutral toward persons and groups, for in the course of growing up we've acquired various beliefs and feelings toward them which, in turn, affect much of what we say and do in our relationships. When we have a favorable attitude toward someone, that person has a reasonable idea of what to expect from us in various situations. Conversely, when we have an unfavorable attitude—an "attitude problem"—toward someone, he or she may find it difficult, if not impossible to satisfy us, no matter what he or she does, because of our attitude.

Attitudes affect our listening behavior in a number of ways, some more obvious than others. First, attitudes may distort

our *perceptions* of people and ideas, especially when we view
people according to stereotypes—faulty generalizations.
When this happens we hear what we *want* to hear or *need* to
hear, rather than what is objectively being expressed. Also,
attitudes create *expectations* about ourselves and others
which predispose us to act in a given way. For instance, when
we admire and trust a speaker, we tend to pay careful
attention to what that person says. In turn, our attentive
behavior encourages that person to speak more freely and
explain more fully. In contrast, when we distrust or dislike
the speaker, we tend to listen more cautiously and judgmen-
tally, thereby putting the speaker on the defensive and
limiting what is said. In both instances, expectations function
as self-fulfilling prophecies, affecting both our own behavior
and in turn, the speaker's behavior in a way that tends to
bring about the expected result. Then too, attitudes and
attitude changes can often *justify* our behavior. Whenever we
act in a manner that contradicts our existing attitudes, the
resulting dissonance may lead us to change our attitudes. For
instance, if we find ourselves not paying attention to someone
to whom we normally do, we may justify our behavior by
saying "The lecture is boring." Such an explanation is usually
more acceptable to us than honestly examining our motives
and admitting that we're simply too tired or too lazy to make
the effort.

Judging the Speaker Prematurely

The most common attitude problem in listening well is being
judgmental—evaluating what people say too quickly, and not
giving them a fair chance to be heard or understood. I once
walked into a police chief's office where a desk placard read,
"DON'T CONFUSE ME WITH THE FACTS, MY MIND IS
MADE UP." Sure enough, he proved to be a highly opinionated person who did all the talking. I was relieved to be there
on official business, and not as someone in trouble with the
law. Afterwards, upon introspection, I discovered that I was

probably prone to the same fault at times. Had I become better acquainted with the chief, I might have found him to be a more complex and reasonable person than indicated by the sign on his desk.

Unfortunately, it is very natural to judge people prematurely, i.e., to evaluate, and to approve or disapprove things from our personal perspective. For instance, if you see a movie, your initial response may be "I liked it" or "I didn't like it." If you ask a friend, that person may say, "I found it interesting" or "I thought it was boring." In other words, our first reaction is to judge things from our own point of view or our attitudes, depending largely on how we're personally affected. Yet, such judgmental responses interfere with good communication.

SELECTED JUDGMENTAL RESPONSES

- Why didn't you say so?
- You shouldn't act like that.
- Look at it this way.
- Now you're on the right track.
- I know why you did that.
- Who gave you that idea?
- Why don't you forget it?
- You can do better than that.

Judgmental responses tend to put speakers on the defensive. As a result, speakers feel apprehensive and begin choosing their thoughts and words more carefully. They're more apt to say things to justify themselves, giving the listener less opportunity to punch holes in their message. In the process, they give us a less full and honest account of what they originally may have intended to say. The effect of judgmental responses on the listeners themselves is no less dramatic. Once poor listeners hear something they disagree with, they begin to tune out the speaker. From that point on, they may become more intent on expressing their own opinion than on listening. While listeners may attribute the failure in communication to speakers, much of the fault lies with the listeners' emotional filters, as described in chapter 2.

Although evaluation has a legitimate place in listening, it comes later in the process. Accordingly, poor listeners evaluate or judge too quickly; the best listeners delay judgment until the full message is heard. *First*, we listen to understand the message. *Then*, we may evaluate what we hear—weighing the evidence, sorting fact from opinion, and rendering sound judgment. Evaluation is especially appropriate when we're listening to extend our knowledge or must reach a decision about some persuasive appeal. Yet even here, each speaker has a right to be heard.

One analysis of communication found that most verbal communication involves five types of responses: evaluative, interpretive, supportive, probing, and understanding. Evaluative or judgmental responses are the most common of all. Interpretive, supportive, and probing responses occur much less frequently and in that order. Understanding responses are the least common. Furthermore, it was found that when someone uses the same type of response at least 40 percent of the time, people see that person as *always* or *characteristically* responding that way.[1]

How would you rate your own listening responses? Can you think of friends or associates who habitually listen in each of these ways? Judgmental listeners respond by saying things like "That's good" or "That's wrong." Interpretive listeners are more likely to say things like "I know why you said that" or "You're saying that to make me feel guilty." Supportive listeners may be quick to agree or sympathize with the speaker, expressing remarks like "You're absolutely right" or "I feel sorry for you." Probing listeners, on the other hand, are more apt to ask "When?" or "Give me an example."

In contrast, understanding listeners employ the techniques of "active" listening and empathic listening to better understand what they hear. For instance, when seeking clarification, the listener might say, "I don't understand what you mean," or "Would you say that again?" or "Could you explain that a bit more?"

Acceptance

Probably the single-most important requirement for good listening is the attitude of acceptance, which is just the opposite of being judgmental. When we are accepting of others, we seek to understand them rather than prematurely judging everything they say. Instead, we're willing to make an active effort to understand. And when there is uncertainty we're inclined to give the speaker the benefit of the doubt until shown otherwise. Showing acceptance toward someone does not necessarily mean we agree with or approve of what that person says or does. Far from it. It simply means we value that individual as a person with inherent worth and dignity who is entitled to his or her own views and, as such, has a right to be heard. Acceptance communicates that we care about the person. At the least, this means extending people who speak to us the common courtesy of listening to what they are saying at the moment without interrupting them. Even more valued is the willingness to hear them out in the face of disagreement and intense emotions. When people feel hurt or injured by our actions, they're less likely to retaliate or initiate a lawsuit if they feel we care about them.

VERBAL EXPRESSIONS OF ACCEPTANCE
- "I'm pleased you could be with us." (warmth)
- "We respect you for calling our attention to this matter today." (immediacy)
- "Losing the contract really hurt." (understanding)
- "We're willing to give you the opportunity." (trust)
- "I respect your opinion, even though I disagree with it." (nonjudgmental)
- "I can see you've spent a lot of time on this." (enhancing)

☐ "We would like to see you succeed." (caring)
☐ "We will work with you on this." (commitment)

Listening with an accepting attitude puts the speaker at ease, instead of on the defensive, as is the case with judgmental listeners. Speakers feel comfortable enough to think out what they want to say and to express themselves freely; the more accepted people feel, the more apt they are to lower their guard, to become honest, and even self-critical. As a result, speakers who are at ease with their thoughts and feelings express themselves even more honestly than if they felt they were under scrutiny. An example might be the fictional television detective Columbo, who characteristically approaches possible murder suspects in a friendly way throughout his investigation. However, as we generally discover by the end of the show, Columbo elicits more damning evidence from his suspects by his disarming approach than would a more aggressive detective with a judgmental approach.

Ordinarily, acceptance is accompanied by feelings of liking and warmth toward others, expressed in all kinds of subtle ways, like the warmth in our voice or smile, but it is also possible to show our acceptance without the presence of such expressions. In fact, an attitude of acceptance becomes even more important in those situations which involve disagreement, criticism, and anger. It is important, however, that our acceptance be real, that it represent our inner attitude. Faking acceptance may make speakers feel even more uncomfortable than an honest admission of our feelings and differences with them. Again, when it comes to good communication, attitude is even more important than technique.

NONVERBAL EXPRESSIONS OF ACCEPTANCE
— Calm, soothing tone of voice
— Animated, smiling facial expression
— Leaning forward, relaxed posture
— Looking directly into the other person's eyes

— Open, welcoming gestures
— Appropriate touching, including handshake
— Sitting or standing at appropriate distance

It is important to realize that none of us is perfectly accepting. Although psychotherapists sometimes aspire to an "unconditional acceptance" of their clients as a way of bringing about personal growth, this remains more of an ideal than achievement in therapy, much less in everyday communication. The truth is, few people are consistently accepting of anyone all of the time. Even close friends, lovers, and spouses vary in their day-to-day acceptance of each other, depending on their shifting needs, moods, and interactions. Ironically, we may exhibit a steadier tolerance, if not acceptance, toward the wider circle of casual friends, co-workers, and even strangers, mostly because of diminished emotional investment in those relationships. In short, we should generally aim to be as accepting as possible, realizing that no one is totally accepting.

A similar idea applies to the content of communication. That is, we're more willing to consider different ideas and views if they aren't too different from our own. "A latitude of acceptance" refers to the range of potentially acceptable positions centered around one's own views. Persuasive appeals that fall outside the listener's usual range tend to fall on deaf ears. Those that fall well within the listener's latitude of acceptance are more likely to be considered.[2]

Self-acceptance

The reluctance to listen to ideas and opinions that differ too much from our own suggests another reason we have difficulty accepting people—a low degree of *self*-acceptance. It is a well-known axiom in clinical practice that the less we have come to terms with something in ourselves, the less accepting we will be of this in others. As Henry Thoreau said, "As long as a man stands in his own way, the whole world seems to stand in his way." Thus, a good way to discover the "blind spots" within ourselves is by noticing what triggers our emotional, judgmental responses to certain people. For instance, suppose I find myself becoming very annoyed at a lecturer who constantly interrupts members of the audience who speak up and ask questions. Mere awareness and dislike of the lecturer's annoying habit may be commendable, but an intense resentment at such rudeness may signal something else, namely projection—the mechanism by which we attribute unacceptable behaviors, feelings, and motives to others. That is, I may judge such lecturer's listening habits all the more harshly because he or she is doing something objectionable of which I myself may be equally guilty, though this insight may not come to me until a later time.

As listeners, we all could benefit from identifying those things that evoke emotional, judgmental responses from us— our emotional filters. Usually, these reflect aspects of our experience that are poorly integrated within our personality. We can identify them by asking ourselves, "What activates my emotional triggers?" and "What makes me overreact to certain people in an irrational manner?" Since each of us has different blind spots, identifying those things that interfere with listening is usually a personal, ongoing learning process. Once we have become aware of such factors, we can make greater allowance for them and listen more objectively.

By the same token, the more we come to terms with ideas, feelings, and traits within ourselves, the more fully we can accept these in others. Here, again, acceptance does not mean blanket approval or resignation to these shortcomings, as much as a realistic acknowledgement that this is the way people are without being too harsh on them or on ourselves. It means being able to affirm ourselves and others as worthwhile, though imperfect persons. In acknowledging our own inadequacies and faults—always easier said than done—we're better able to deal with those of others in a more rational and constructive manner.

Just as acceptance of people doesn't imply blanket approval of them or what they say, self-acceptance doesn't mean resigning ourselves to our shortcomings, including our faulty listening habits. It does mean acknowledging them as ours rather than something that merely exists in others. Self-acceptance also implies greater ability to listen to ourselves. For instance, whenever we feel ourselves becoming anxious or emotionally aroused, we need to become aware that such a state interferes with our ability to listen. Similarly, when we find ourselves overreacting to someone in a judgmental manner, it's best to acknowledge this at least to ourselves, if not to others, as a way of keeping the channels of communication open. Keener awareness of these tendencies may motivate us to make greater strides in self-improvement. Our goal should be steady improvement in these matters, since complete self-acceptance, like the acceptance of others, remains an ideal.

The attitude of acceptance, as discussed throughout this chapter, implies an overall receptiveness to people, a willingness to consider their ideas and feelings. Effective listening depends as much, if not more, on the attitude of acceptance as it does on the mastery of specific listening techniques. In their book on *Managing Human Resources*, Leonard Sayles and George Strauss point out that the listening approach is not something to be applied only when dealing with specific problems: "It is a general attitude which the manager can apply day in and day out in dealings with fellow supervisors, subordinates, and the boss. Having an accepting attitude means always being ready to listen to the other person's view and trying to take it into account before taking action oneself."[3]

9

The Risks and Rewards of Listening

When the Ford Motor Company, like other American car manufacturers, saw Americans driving Japanese-made cars, they realized it was time to change their ways. Donald E. Peterson, then chairman of Ford, became convinced that if the company wasn't "customer-driven," their cars wouldn't be either. Consequently, he emphasized the importance of listening to customers at all levels, and Ford employees began listening to groups of car owners. The results shook Ford into action. As a result, more consumers than ever were invited to evaluate the prototypes of the Taurus and Sable models. When consumers complained that the rear seat area lacked foot room, Ford sloped the floor underneath the front seats, widened the space between seat-adjustment tracks, and made the tracks out of smooth plastic instead of metal. Buyers have rewarded Ford for such efforts by record sales of both of these models. Now Ford surveys over two million of its customers each year and also invites owners to meet with dealers and engineers to discuss problems of quality.[1]

The importance of listening is part of a renewed interest in customer satisfaction. But wise managers are not simply touting money-back guarantees and service with a smile, important as these are. They're also talking about reorganizing entire companies around giving consumers what they want from research to the end product. There is new evidence that companies that listen well and respond promptly thrive financially as well. In fact, some consultants have developed a model for measuring the dollars-and-cents value of retaining customers through providing better service.[2]

At the same time, the emphasis on listening, like the introduction of any change in the workplace, usually involves a consideration of the cost/benefit ratio. That is, the expected benefits of a given course of action are weighed against its anticipated costs. In listening, as in all human endeavors, the net benefits should outweigh the costs involved. Throughout much of this book, I have mentioned the risks of *not* listening and the costly mistakes this often entails, but I can also list some risks, as well as rewards, in the act of listening itself.

The Risks of Listening

You may be surprised to discover that listening may in some instances be risky, but it's true. Let us consider some of the major risks of listening, and why people may avoid listening, consciously or unconsciously.

Listening may result in information overloads and confusion. Listening, like other perceptions, is selective. That is, we attend to certain things and not others, mostly on the basis of what appears to be interesting and useful to us. However, there's ample evidence that we naturally tend to hear things we need or want to hear, thereby prematurely filtering out other aspects of reality. By contrast, if we make the effort, really listening to others may bring us more accurate information and understanding. Also, by listening to more than one person, including those who disagree with us, we may get a more objective picture of a situation. However, in the process, there is the risk that we will experience information overload and hear more than we can meaningfully handle at the time. As a result, we may become troubled or confused.

Listening makes us vulnerable to the deeper concerns and problems of others. Ordinarily, we feel we have enough on our minds with our personal affairs without listening to others. When we do listen to them, we become aware of their inner lives, their problems, frustrations, and hurts. The more we listen to people, the more emotionally involved with them we become. In turn, this makes us more vulnerable to their potential demands on us. The combination of their problems and our own may overburden us. Hence, the common practice of distancing ourselves from others. Then too, since empathic listening requires an emotional concern without excessive involvement, there is always the danger that we may exceed our tolerance for emotional involvement.

Listening increases our risk of hearing criticism. Perhaps this is why we listen so selectively in the first place. Ordinarily, when we have worked so hard to achieve or create something, we become so emotionally involved with it that we are not prepared to hear it criticized. Criticism makes us anxious and defensive; we feel we're being personally attacked. Yet genuinely listening increases our risk of hearing criticism. As one mother put it, if you really listen to your kids, be prepared to hear some things you do not want to hear. This is simply part of good communication. In fact, if you are in any position of authority or intimacy and are only hearing pleasant things, you should question how well you're communicating. In business, subordinates are reluctant to convey problems or bad news because of the "kill-the-messenger-of-bad-news" syndrome. A good listener always assumes the risk of hearing and absorbing the bad news along with the good.

Listening heightens the risk of seeing ourselves as others see us. Each of us has built up certain images of ourselves. Some of these images are fairly realistic, others are less so. When speaking, we tend to present ourselves in a favorable manner. But when we listen, we run the risk of hearing things that conflict with our self-image. Unflattering views are difficult to hear, much less to accept. As William James once said, "Whenever two people meet, there are really six people present. There is each person as he sees himself, each person as the other sees him, and each person as he really is." Listening to criticism as well as compliments, hard as it may be, helps us to see ourselves as we *really* are.

Our willingness to listen may be unappreciated, time-consuming, and exploited. Most everyone wants to be heard and understood. This is what makes friends, lovers, and spouses so valued—they're willing to listen to us. People going through severe crises in their lives often agree to pay someone like a psychiatrist, psychologist, or marriage counselor to listen to them. Short of this, these people are responsive to genuine listening on the part of anyone at hand. Yet, individuals who are emotionally aroused or deeply hurt may be so blinded by thier emotions that they make unreasonable demands on anyone who cares enough to listen to them. Then there are the compulsive talkers who express their insecurity and need for control through excessive talking. They dominate the conversation in a way that makes it practically impossible to really listen to them. Experience with these people soon teaches us that being a martyr does not make us good listeners. Rather, listening is hard work and should be done selectively.

In listening to everyone else's views we may fail to give sufficient credit to our own. Like everything else, listening can be strained to the point where it is counterproductive. This is especially so when there are several conflicting views on a controversial issue. Up to a point, listening helps people to air their opinions. Beyond that, endless attempts to listen often needlessly prolong a discussion and may lead to a stalemate rather than the action or decision that is needed. At some point, those in a position of leadership must contribute their own judgment and move things ahead. Then too, if you are in a sales meeting, for example, and are trying to develop your position on a plan or issue, listening to too many other views may divert your focus away from a really creative option.

Listening to Criticism

Nowhere is our listening ability put to the test as much as in listening to criticism. Just think for a moment. How do you feel when you are criticized? Do you feel threatened? Do you feel resentful, even when you're wrong? When people are asked to complete the statement "When I am criticized, . . ." typical responses include "I get upset," "I resent it," and "I wonder when the axe will fall." Such comments suggest that we take criticism as a personal attack against which we must defend ourselves at all cost. Consequently, we waste energy worrying about criticism, needlessly justifying ourselves, and going to great lengths to avoid it.

Yet, listening to criticism can become a valuable means toward improvement and personal growth. For instance, there were also some positive answers to the above statement. One man said, "Criticism tells me where the other person is coming from and how she sees me." A woman said, "When I'm criticized, I try to figure out what they are trying to tell me, and how I can improve my work." These people have acquired the valuable art of learning from criticism.

In the bestseller *Nobody's Perfect*, Hendrie Weisinger and Norman Lobsenz suggest three ways we can learn from criticism. Each strategy centers around one of the three basic aspects of personality—our thoughts, feelings, and behavior.[3]

First, view criticism as a valuable source of new information to be evaluated objectively. We don't have to rush out and change something each time we are criticized. Instead, each criticism should be taken as a cue that *may* require action. You might ask yourself, "What is this person trying to tell me?" and *"How important* is this criticism?" The more important the information is to you, the more likely you need to do something about it. Then too, consider *how often* a particular criticism is offered. If you're frequently criticized for the same behavior by different people, there's a good chance the criticism is valid and should be acted upon. Furthermore, consider the *source* of criticism. People often feel they are being criticized unfairly, especially when the other person is under a lot of stress. By contrast, the more qualified someone is to judge your work, the more you should take the criticism to heart. Even criticism spoken in frustration and anger may need to be heeded, taking into account the exaggeration due to emotions. Finally, you need to weigh the *pros and cons of acting* on a criticism. Do the benefits that come from acting on the criticism balance or outweigh the effort involved? For instance, a worker called in for a performance review may wonder whether or not to take the additional training suggested by her supervisor. Doing so will entail extra time and effort on her part but could also lead to improved performance. On the other hand, the failure to act on the supervisor's suggestion may jeopardize her advancement, if not the job itself.

Second, put the emotional energy aroused by criticism to work for you, not against you. Emotional arousal tends to interfere with our ability to perform well. In fact, the more sophisticated and technical the task, the greater the interference. Consequently, when you're criticized, try to stay calm. Relax physically. Remind yourself that nobody is trying to hurt you. Instead, what this person is saying will probably be helpful. Then use your emotions as a source of energy to make the necessary change. For example, each time Carol did something her husband disliked, he would yell, "That's stupid" or "How dumb can you be?" Carol would become upset and try to ignore his accusations as a way of justifying her actions. Gradually Carol learned to remain calm in the face of Bob's outbursts. She would ask, "What is it you're objecting to?" or "How would you suggest handling this?" Responding in kind, Bob learned to give more specific criticisms, which Carol found more helpful.

Third, take positive steps to put the needed changes into action. Don't waste energy defending yourself. Instead, listen carefully to what is being said. Ask for more information. Ask the person for suggested solutions to the criticism. You might ask for this indirectly, such as, "If you were in my place, what would you do?" Or you might ask more directly, "What would you like me to do?" People usually criticize something we're doing, but it often comes across as a personal attack because many people do not know how to give criticism constructively. So if someone says, "You're rude and inconsiderate," ask them, "In what ways have I been inconsiderate?" In this way, you'll focus on something tangible, which in due time may lead to the desired changes in your self-image and reputation.

A successful executive once told me, "Your critics can tell you where you are going wrong even before your friends can." Apparently, he had learned the folk wisdom attributed to the famous philosopher Leibnitz: "I would walk twenty miles to listen to my worst enemy if I could learn something." Listening to criticism may deflate the ego momentarily, but the failure to listen can be even more costly.

The Rewards of Listening

More often than not, the risks of listening are more than offset by its rewards. Consider the following rewards of listening.

Effective listening provides us with information and understanding. In an age of spectacular electronic advances, we are constantly bombarded with information, from television, fax machines, newspapers, and telephones to all other sorts of media. Yet, because of poor attending skills, much of this information "goes in one ear and out the other." Effective listening can help us to process this information more efficiently and more accurately. The use of "active" listening skills in conversation leads to better understanding. And the more we understand something, the better we retain it. Consequently, the way to know more is to listen more effectively.

Empathic listening gives us a better understanding of other people. A major cause of misunderstanding between people is our tendency to judge each other on the basis of too little information. Listening helps to counteract this common tendency. When we listen empathically, we are more apt to see things from someone else's perspective. We come to realize that the meaning of someone's behavior is more complex than it often appears. More especially, to a greater extent than we realize, that behavior is influenced by circumstances. Then too, through empathic listening, we may learn how people feel about themselves and why they act the way they do. Empathic listening helps us to take into account people's needs and intentions.

Listening facilitates good communication. As we noted earlier, communication involves more than words and information, having also to do with the expression of personal meanings, attitudes, and feelings, often encoded in socially acceptable ways. Thus, we need to use "active" listening skills in order to learn what others are really trying to say to us. We also need to give them feedback to acknowledge that we understand them. When people feel we are listening to them they are more likely to adopt a favorable impresssion of us. Also, once we've listened to them, they in turn are more likely to listen to us. Consequently, listening facilitates a *mutual* exchange of information, feelings, and understanding, which is the essence of good communication.

Listening facilitates self-discovery. Through listening to others we learn to listen to ourselves. We become aware of attitudes, feelings, and needs of which we were only dimly aware before. Listening may also help to broaden the images we have of ourselves. We may discover that people see us as more competent or attractive than we realize. Sometimes, though, we will hear less flattering things, which may make us anxious or resentful. But listening to criticism may be the most helpful of all kinds of listening, especially when it is well intended. Even when it's given in anger, criticism may bring needed awareness of our mistakes and shortcomings. When taken to heart, such understanding can become a valuable aid to self-discovery and can improve our relationships with others.

Listening is worth the time it takes in reaching better decisions and solving problems. Decisions and solutions to problems are only as good as the information upon which they are based. Listening helps us to process information more efficiently, to become aware of the underlying issues as well as the surface symptoms, and to reach more satisfying solutions. Also, listening helps us to make use of criticism and conflict in reaching the best decision, in both individual relationships and groups.

For instance L. L. Bean, Inc., the well-known mail-order company, discovered that in 1988 its customers had returned $82 million worth of merchandise. That represented 14 percent of Bean's total sales, not to mention the $2 million in return freight charges. Because about two-thirds of the returns involved wrong sizes, management asked for the employees' help in solving this problem. The employees recommended improving the size information provided in the catalog as well as some changes in the order-takers' computers. Bean also retrained 3,200 employees in techniques that would boost customer service and quality. Consequently, when dissatisfied customers called about exchanging goods, the order-takers listened with extra care to make certain the correct sizes were sent out.[4]

Finally, listening leads to better management. The higher one goes in the chain of responsibility in business or other domains, the more one's job has to do with people and human relations. The most effective style of management, often called "team management,' is one which has the optimal balance between the goals of production and the needs of people. This managerial viewpoint takes into consideration that the needs of today's workforce are different from those of earlier eras. Today's managers realize that customers and workers need to be heard. When people take part in planning their work, they tend to be committed to getting it done and work at a higher level of motivation. When people are committed to their work, they also exert self-control, which, in turn, is likely to lead to higher productivity. Such a management style helps to build an organizational climate of trust, respect, and open communication.[5]

Today, people in positions of management, in addition to their special knowledge and expertise in a given line of work, must also become a special kind of people, adept in dealing with human relations. "The development of oneself as a listener," says Carl Rogers, "is a first step in becoming this special person."[6] Good listening is appropriate for a variety of purposes:

- → Interviewing: especially for hiring, firing, and making transfers.
- → Motivating employees: discovering the causes of dissatisfaction, absenteeism, or turnovers.
- → Improving instruction: Insuring that people understand instructions, as well as getting reaction and acceptance.
- → Overcoming resistance to change: Gaining acceptance of new techniques and procedures.
- → Evaluating: Discovering how employees are performing and helping them to correct their weaknesses.
- → Settling disputes: Finding out the causes of disputes between employees and helping them to reach a settlement.[7]

To this list we would add the all-important area of customer service from the L. L. Bean example given above. This includes, of course, hearing and heeding the questions, problems, and complaints of the people who keep the company in business by buying its products.

Whether you are in a business, school, home, or other kind of environment, there are both risks and rewards in listening. But more often than not, the rewards of listening will more than offset the potential risks. As Calvin Coolidge, former president of the United States, reminded us, "Nobody ever listened himself out of a job."

10

You Can Become an Effective Listener

B y now you should be well aware that listening, unlike hearing, is a learned skill. Even though many people listen poorly, it is usually because they have learned to listen that way. By the same token, each of us can improve our listening skills through such endeavors as reading books, playing audio or video cassettes on the subject, attending seminars or workshops on listening, and taking courses in speech communication that include modules on listening.

The Good Listener

At this point, try visualizing yourself as an effective listener. Close your eyes and imagine, as vividly as you can, the kind of listener you'd like to become with someone you know. Visualize yourself being attentive. Look at this person as she speaks. Nod your head or smile occasionally. Picture yourself "actively" listening as you reflect her feelings as well as the content of her message. You are patiently hearing her out.

Imagining yourself as the listener you want to become may help you not only to attain your goal but also to function more effectively in the present.[1]

Also, you might find it helpful to think of the best listeners you know. How would you describe their listening habits? When Robert L. Montgomery posed this question, he learned what people said about the good listener:

▢ Looks at me while I'm speaking
▢ Questions me to clarify what I'm saying
▢ Shows concern by asking questions about my feelings
▢ Repeats some of the things I say
▢ Doesn't rush me
▢ Is poised and emotionally controlled
▢ Reacts responsively with a nod, a frown, or a smile
▢ Pays close attention
▢ Doesn't interrupt me
▢ Keeps on the subject until I've finished my thoughts.[2]

Notice how different these characteristics are from those in the comparable list of the poor listener's habits presented in chapter 1. For instance, the good listener "doesn't rush me" or "interrupt me," whereas the poor listener "jumps to conclusions," "finishes my sentences" and "changes the subject."

Also observe that the characteristics of good listeners reflect much of what we've discussed throughout this book. For example, the good listener "pays close attention," a hallmark of effective listening. "Looks at me while I'm speaking" reminds us of the importance of total body listening.

"Reacts responsively with a nod, a frown, or a smile" illustrates those minimal responses that enhance the flow of conversation. "Clarifies what I am saying, repeating some of the things I say" and "asking questions about my feelings" are examples of the "active" listening skills—clarifying, paraphrasing, summarizing, and reflecting feelings.

Note, too, that the good listener "is poised and emotionally controlled," suggesting an awareness of his of her own emotional filters, an indispensable aid to listening objectively. Finally, the good listener "keeps on the subject until I've finished my thoughts," showing forbearance and the willingness to hear people out as in "active" and empathic listening.

EFFECTIVE LISTENING SKILLS
✔ Paying attention to the speaker
✔ "Active" listening to ensure accuracy

✔ Adopting an accepting attitude
✔ Allowing the speaker ample time
✔ Staying on the subject
✔ Making retrieval responses when you interrupt
✔ Being aware of your emotional reactions

The question is, how motivated are you to become an effective listener? Are you personally convinced that it pays to listen? Each of us must answer this question.

Furthermore, we must make a *decision* to change. For example, it is only when a wish to change leads to a decision to change that we really change and grow. For instance, many smokers dislike their smoking habit. They say things such as "I'd *like* to stop smoking" and "I *hope* to give it up one day" and "I *plan* to cut down on smoking." But until they *decide* to stop smoking and learn how to implement that decision, nothing happens.

Changing Your Listening Style

Learning to listen more effectively involves four stages: (1) Becoming aware, (2) Internalizing, (3) Practicing, and (4) Integrating.

In the initial stage, individuals become keenly *aware* of their listening habits. This may result from frustration in their communication with others at work or at home, or it may come from reading an article or book about listening, such as this one. The particular habits in question will vary from one person to another, whether it be a tendency to listen in an emotional and judgmental manner, turning ordinary conversations into arguments, or habitually interrupting others, thereby frustrating speakers and dominating the conversation. As our awareness progresses we may feel somewhat sheepish if not inadequate about our poor listening habits.

Also, if we're honest with ourselves, we may find ourselves resisting change. Realizing that we don't listen very well may be upsetting, but it may not be sufficiently so to cause us to do anything about it. Only as we examine the cost/benefits ratio and become personally motivated will we initiate change. We may prefer to stick with our habitual ways of listening mostly because they are familiar, in the same way that old shoes are more comfortable than new ones.

The second stage in learning to listen more effectively is the stage of *internalizing*, in which we actively acquire new, more effective listening skills. At this stage, people are busy rereading the book and applying what they've learned. For instance, they may begin to practice active listening skills with their friends or colleagues. Or, they may enroll in a course or seminar as a way of getting more direction and help in modifying their listening habits. For instance, my college offers an introductory course in speech communication, which generally covers speaking, listening, and small group work. Many books have now been written on the value of sharpening our listening skills in both business and personal environments. Consultants and professionals offer workshops and courses nationwide on listening and spoken communication.

In the third stage effective listening *skills are practiced* regularly. We have begun to experience the benefits of "active" listening skills, but realize we need more practice.

At this point it helps to get some observations from others. One way is to ask another person such as a close friend, colleague, lover, or spouse to give you feedback. Ask them to share something they really want to communicate, and practice your active listening skills, such as clarifying, paraphrasing, summarizing, and reflecting feelings. Then ask them to give you an honest appraisal of how well you listened. If you are reading this book as part of a seminar or group interested in improving your listening skills, you can do the following in pairs. One person expresses a concern or problem for five minutes and the other person practices listening. Then reverse the roles.

Still another way is to form triads. One person is the

speaker, one the listener, and the third is the observer. The speaker should begin by sharing a felt concern or problem. Then the listener practices "active" listening skills. After about five minutes, the observer calls time, then points out two or three positive things about the listener's performance and as many (or fewer) constructive criticisms, preferably accompanied by suggestions for improvement. For example, the observer might say, "You waited too long before responding. It might help to give the speaker some feedback sooner or more frequently." Then rotate the roles until each person has had an opportunity to play each role.

In the fourth and final stage, we are incorporating effective listening skills into our habitual manner of communicating. In many ways, this is more of an ideal or a long-range aim for most of us, since learning to listen well can remain a lifelong goal. Even professional therapists need periodic reminders. For instance, as a teacher and therapist I should be in this integrating stage, yet I find that I'm constantly becoming aware of ways in which I don't listen well. It's the old saying: The more you know the more you realize how much there still is to learn. Thus, the more accomplished you become in an area, the more aware you are of the need for constant improvement. I find that teaching and supervising others in listening skills helps me to see my own need for improvement. For example, after a class, I may realize that I have cut a person short, sometimes because of time limitations, and must work to avoid this discourtesy in the future. Or, in personal conversation I become aware of interrupting someone, or switching the topic rather than trying to make a retrieval to the original topic.

There is no necessary time requirement for mastering these stages; it's more a matter of practice and experience. After reading a book or attending a workshop on listening, most people take several weeks or months reaching the practicing stage—usually longer. A lot depends on their access to workshops, courses, and supervision. Also, it is

Stages of Modifying Your Listening Style

These stages are best understood as overlapping steps involving varying intervals of time depending on the individual and such factors as personal motivation, learning experience, and feedback.

1. Becoming Aware

Increased awareness of your listening habits, along with the desire to change.

2. Internalizing

Initiated by the decision to modify your listening behavior and acquire more effective listening skills.

3. Practicing

Characterized by regular practice of effective listening skills, aided by self-evaluation and feedback from others.

4. Integrating

Habitual and unconscious use of effective listening skills, accompanied by lifelong improvement in listening.

important to take advantage of everyday opportunities to practice your listening skills. You might select one or two friends on whom you can try out your skills.

Some Dos and Don'ts of Listening

There have been many principles and techniques presented throughout the book for improving your listening habits. Now, partly as a way of summarizing them, here are some simple rules for becoming a better listener. While many of these suggestions pertain to a specific act, such as paying attention, others involve a change in attitude or motivation. All of them require repeated practice for mastery. As you practice your new skills, it will be helpful to refer back to these rules.

When listening, try to *do* the following:

1. Be aware of your own listening habits. What are your strong points? What are your particular weaknesses? Are you habitually inattentive, having to ask others to repeat what they've said? Do you jump to conclusions? Do you interrupt? Are you improving your listening habits? Awareness of your listening habits is the first stage in changing them.

2. Pay attention to the speaker. Due to our short attention spans, listening requires concentration. Then too, because we can listen at a much faster rate than people can speak, our minds wander. Even the best listeners find their awareness alternately "going away" and "coming back" to the speaker's words. Consequently, to listen well, you must make a constant effort to attend to the speaker and keep "coming back" to what is being said.

3. Share responsibility for the communication. Most of the meaning in a conversation is filled in by the person listening. Thus, we need to use "active" listening skills to make certain we understand what the speaker is actually saying. Whenever something is unclear, resist the temptation to blame the speaker. Instead, ask for clarification or pose questions.

4. Be physically attentive. Face the speaker. Maintain appropriate eye contact—alternately looking at the speaker and looking away. Make certain your posture and gestures show you're listening. Sit or stand at a comfortable distance that puts you and the speaker at ease. Remember, people want an attentive, animated listener, not a passive audience.

5. Listen for the total meaning being communicated. Keep in mind that communication involves more than information. People are actively attempting to express their attitudes, understandings, and feelings, though these are generally "encoded" in socially acceptable ways. Use "active" listening skills to check the accuracy of your understanding. Listen to what people say, but also find out how they feel.

6. Express empathic understanding. Try to put yourself in the other person's shoes and find out what they are saying from their own personal frame of reference. Discuss what is important to the speaker. Use "active" listening skills. Reflect the speaker's expressed feelings, rather than saying "I understand how you feel." Empathic listening not only creates rapport with others, but it also gives us a more accurate understanding of their intended message.

7. Observe the speaker's nonverbal signals. Since much communication is nonverbal, pay attention to the speaker's body language as well as the words. Does the speaker establish eye contact with you, or not? Listen to the person's tone of voice and rate of speech. Notice how close or far away the speaker sits or stands from you. Does the speaker's body language reinforce or contradict the spoken words? When in doubt, nonverbal behavior often provides the decisive clue.

8. Adopt an accepting attitude toward the speaker. Remember, we tend to judge people prematurely. In contrast, an accepting attitude on the listener's part creates a favorable atmosphere for communication. Speakers who feel accepted can let down their guard and express themselves more freely. By contrast, negative attitudes on the listener's part tend to put the speaker on the defensive.

9. Listen to yourself. Are you generally calm and receptive to what people are saying to you, or do your emotions frequently get in the way? When we become anxious or emotionally aroused, we tend to tune out what people are saying to us. At the same time, when you think it will help to clear the air, express your feelings in a socially acceptable manner.

10. "Close the loop" of listening by taking appropriate action. People generally speak to us with some purpose in mind. Sometimes it is mostly to share their ideas or feelings with us. At other times they want to obtain information or to get us to do something. The acid test of listening is how well we respond to the speaker's message with appropriate action. In listening, as in love, actions speaker louder than words.

Although the emphasis should be on positive suggestions for improving our listening habits, it may be helpful to keep in mind some of the major pitfalls of this process.

Consequently, in listening, *don't* do the following:

1. Don't interrupt needlessly. This is the major sign of poor listening. People in positions of power, such as parents, teachers, managers, and executives are the worst offenders. If you must interrupt someone in a serious conversation, try to follow with a retrieval response—helping to reestablish the speaker's train of thought. Switching the subject of a conversation without mutual agreement is rude.

2. Don't mistake not talking for listening. When we remain silent we aren't necessarily listening. We may simply be awaiting our turn to speak. Meanwhile, our thoughts tend to stray. We become preoccupied with what we want to say or our reactions to the speaker's message. At the same time, our inattentiveness usually shows in our facial expression and body language. It is hard to fake listening.

3. Don't blame the speaker for failures in communication. Despite popular opinion, the speaker does not bear the overwhelming responsibility for communication. It takes two to communicate—one to talk and another to listen. Keep in mind that the listener shares responsibility for the communication. When you misunderstand someone, ask yourself— Did I provide sufficient feedback? Did I ask questions? Was I listening actively?

4. Don't listen passively. Most speakers want an animated listener. Are you physically attentive? Do you offer those brief facilitative responses, such as "mm-hm," "yeah," and "really?" that keep the flow of conversation going? Do you use "active" listening skills? Do you try to put yourself in the speaker's shoes in order to understand what he or she is saying?

5. Don't ask too many questions. While an occasional question helps to clarify what is being said, too many questions become distracting. Emphasize open-ended questions that encourage the speaker to elaborate on his or her message. The use of closed questions should be kept to a minimum. An overreliance on questions tends to shift control of the conversation to the listener, putting the speaker on the defensive.

6. Don't assume too much. Instead, use "active" listening skills to provide the speaker with feedback of what you've heard. When in doubt, clarify vague or ambivalent messages. Even when you think you understand, paraphrase the speaker's message in your own words as a way of checking on the accuracy of your understanding. Summarizing responses, especially in meetings, remind everyone of what has been said up to that point.

7. Don't ever tell someone "I know exactly how you feel." Such a generalized response is likely to distract the speaker from further expressions of his or her feelings. Furthermore, it casts doubt on your own credibility as a listener. It is usually more effective to *demonstrate* you have heard with a reflective, empathic response such as "You are feeling disappointed," "You're feeling hurt," or whatever feelings have been expressed.

8. Don't pass judgment too quickly. We have a natural

tendency to judge, to evaluate, and to approve or disapprove what is said—all of which interfere with accurate listening and understanding. Also, such judgmental responses invariably put a speaker on the defensive and serve as barriers to good communication. By contrast, an accepting attitude generally encourages the speaker to express himself or herself more freely.

9. *Don't become defensive in the face of criticism.* It's a waste of time. Instead, put the energy of emotional arousal to work for you. Ask yourself, What is this person trying to tell me? How important is it? Does this require aciton or not? If so, ask your critics for their suggestions. They can usually tell you where you're going wrong even before your friends can.

10. *Don't use listening as a way of hiding yourself.* Insecure people tend to rely on passive listening as a way of avoiding self-disclosure. They withhold their own views or feelings for fear of disapproval or criticism. By contrast, genuine communication involves animated listeners and the *mutual* expression of opinions. In a satisfying conversation, all participants share the listening and speaking roles.

Listening well does not preclude expressing your own thoughts and feelings. It has more to do with restoring the balance of communication. As a store clerk once said to me, "Everybody wants to talk. Nobody wants to listen." She's right, because our society overvalues talking compared to the lost art of listening. But effective listening is indispensable to good communication, and, as we've seen, it must be learned. It takes time and effort. Yet when all is said and done, what can be more gratifying than hearing someone out and experiencing the appreciation that comes with it? Or, conversely, what is more satisfying than to have someone return the favor by listening and understanding you? Listening becomes a way of showing that we care about each other.

Notes

1. Whatever Happened to Listening?

1. Marcey Grothe and Peter Wylie, *Problem Bosses: Who They Are and How to Deal With Them*. New York: Fawcett, 1987.

2. *Your Personal Listening Profile*. Sperry Corporation, 1980.

3. Robert L. Montgomery, *Listening Made Easy*. New York: AMACOM, 1981, pp. 14–15.

4. V. O. Jenks, *Human Relations in Organizations*. New York: Harper & Row, 1990.

5. Ron Adler and Neil Towne, *Looking Out/Looking In*. San Francisco: Rinehart Press, 1975.

6. From *Go Ask Alice*. Englewood Cliffs, N.J.: Prentice Hall, 1971.

7. *The Philadelphia Inquirer*, "They Got Rid of the Bum—as well as His $1 Million." February 21, 1989, p. 3A.

2. How You Became the Listener You Are

1. Gail Gregg, "They Have Ears, But Hear Not." *Personal Growth and Behavior*, 91/92. Guilford, CT: The Dushkin Publishing Group, 1991, pp. 157–60.

2. *The Philadelphia Inquirer.* April 22, 1991, p. 1D.

3. *Register Report.* Council for the National Register of Health Service Providers in Psychology, Vol. 16, no. 4, 1991.

4. Elizabeth Start, "Wild Blue Blunders." *Psychology Today,* October 1988, pp. 30–33.

5. V. O. Jenks, *Human Relations in Organizations.* New York: Harper & Row, 1990.

6. Marcey Grothe and Peter Wylie, *Problem Bosses: Who They Are and How to Deal With Them.* New York: Fawcett, 1987.

3. Learning to Listen

1. Lyman K. Steil, Larry L. Barker, and Kittie W. Watson, *Effective Listening.* New York: Random House, 1983, pp. 5–6.

2. Steil, Barker, and Watson, p. 19.

3. Deborah Tannen, *You Just Don't Understand.* New York: William Morrow, 1990, p. 37.

4. Associated Press, *The Philadelphia Inquirer,* November 27, 1980.

5. *Your Personal Listening Profile.* Sperry Corporation, 1980.

4. Conversational Listening

1. Nathan Miller, quoted in Robert Bolton, *People Skills.* Englewood Cliffs, NJ: Prentice Hall, 1979, p. 4.

2. Deborah Tannen, *You Just Don't Understand*. New York: William Morrow, 1990.

3. Tannen, pp. 188–215.

4. Tannen, p. 188.

5. "Active" Listening Skills

1. William H. Cormier and L. Sherilyn Cormier, *Interview Strategies for Helpers*, 3rd ed. Belmont, CA: Brooks/ Cole Publishing Company, 1991, pp. 89–91.

2. Ibid., pp. 92–94.

3. Ibid., pp. 100–103.

6. Empathic Listening

1. Carl Rogers, *A Way of Being*. Boston: Houghton Mifflin, 1980.

2. L. M. Brammer, E. L. Shostrom, and P. J. Abrego, *Therapeutic Psychology*, 5th ed. Englewood Cliffs, NJ: Prentice Hall, 1989.

3. N. Eisenberg and R. Lennon, "Sex Differences in Empathy and Related Capacities." *Psychological Bulletin*. 1983, pp. 100–131.

4. William H. Cormier and L. Sherilyn Cormier, *Interview Strategies for Helpers*, 3rd ed. Belmont, CA: Brooks/ Cole Publishing Company, 1991, pp. 22–23.

5. Ibid., pp. 95–99.

6. G. Egan, *The Skilled Helper*, 4th ed. Pacific Grove, CA: Brooks/Cole Publishing Company, 1990.

7. L. Sherilyn Cormier and Harold Hackney, *The Professional Counselor*. Englewood Cliffs, NJ: Prentice Hall, 1987, pp. 45–48.

8. A. Hammer, "Matching Perceptual Predicates: Effect on Perceived Empathy in a Counseling Analogue." *Journal of Counseling Psychology*, 1983, 30, pp. 172–79.

7. Nonverbal Communication

1. Julius Fast, *Body Language*. New York: M. Evans and Company, Inc. 1970.

2. R. Rosenthal, et al., "Body Talk and Tone of Voice: The Language Without Words." *Psychology Today*. September 1974, pp. 64–68.

3. P. Ekman, W. V. Friesen, and P. Ellsworth, *Emotion in the Human Face*. New York: Pergamon Press, 1972.

4. Rollo May, *Love and Will*. New York: Dell Publishing Company, 1974, p. 239.

5. John Lamberth, *Social Psychology*. New York: Macmillan Publishing Company, 1980.

6. E. A. Hall, "A System for the Notation of Proxemic Behavior." *American Anthropologist*. 1963, pp. 1003–26.

7. Lamberth, *Social Psychology*.

8. Attitude Is All-Important

1. David W. Johnson, *Reaching Out*. Englewood Cliffs, NJ: Prentice Hall, 1972.

2. A. Atkins, K. Deaux, and J. Bieri, "Latitude of Acceptance and Attitude Change: Empirical Evidence for a

Reformulation." *Journal of Personality and Social Psychology*, 1967, 6, 47–54.

3. Leonard R. Sayles and George Strauss, *Managing Human Resources*, 2nd ed. Englewood Cliffs, NJ: Prentice Hall, 1981, p. 114.

9. The Risks and Rewards of Listening

1. Stephen Phillips, Amy Dunkin, James B. Treece, and Keith H. Hammonds, "King Customer." *Business Week*, March 12, 1990, pp. 88–94.

2. Ibid.

3. Hendrie Weisinger and Norman M. Lobsenz, *Nobody's Perfect*. New York: Warner Books, 1981.

4. Phillips, Dunkin, Treece, and Hammonds, p. 94.

5. V. O. Jenks, *Human Relations in Organizations*, New York: Harper & Row, 1990.

6. Norman B. Sigband, *Communication for Management and Business*, 2nd ed. Glenview, IL: Scott, Foresman and Company, 1976, p. 576.

7. Leonard R. Sayles and George Strauss, *Managing Human Resources*, 2nd ed. Englewood Cliffs, NJ: Prentice Hall, 1981.

10. You Can Become an Effective Listener

1. P. Adelman, "Possibly Yours." *Psychology Today*. April 1988, pp. 8, 10.

2. Robert L. Montgomery, *Listening Made Easy*. New York: AMACOM, 1981, p. 15.

Index